As you spend time in each day's study, you will come to know in an Christ's love for you. Sharon does a masterful job of unpacking the Scripture with insights and revelations that may have otherwise gone better, this book is for you. If you want to know how very much He loves you, this book is for you. you will truly not want to miss a day. It is a resource that you will go back to again and again. I have. I wish I could better express on paper the impact this book has had on me. So grateful that Sharon was obedient to the Holy Spirit in writing *Loved*.

Fern Nichols, Founder of Moms in Prayer International

You will love this study on the Book of John! Sharon writes from the overflow of her time spent with Jesus and her time in the Word of God. She has this beautiful balance of being real as well as being true to what God has to say to us. We are loved! Each one of us will walk away from this study knowing this truth in the depths of our souls. May we all be transformed because of this simple fact: nothing can change His love for us. His love is based on Him and not on us. Thank you, Sharon, for writing a study that will absolutely change lives for eternity!

Nancy Lindgren, Founder and CEO, MORE Mentoring

From the first introduction sentences, Sharon captivates us with the story of John. Each day is very intentionally designed with her 4R Method to help keep our eyes on Jesus and what He is saying to us in this amazing book of the Bible. Her 4R Method for studying God's Word brings what we read to new depths and understanding. This book will renew your quiet time with Jesus!

Bonnie Nichols, Founder, Wholehearted

If you are looking for a Bible study that draws you closer to the Lord, this is it! Loved is a compelling study to help you develop your love relationship with the Lord. The content and homework are focused on growing our understanding of Jesus Christ and how much He loves each one of us individually. This study—with homework focused on reading and reflecting on the Gospel of John—is life-giving for those new to the faith as well as those who have been Christians for many years. And if you're looking for a way to establish a regular time in God's Word, this study will help you do just that.

Cyndie Claypool de Neve, Marriage & Family Therapist,
Author of *God-Confident Kids*

I've been a pastor now for over 25 years and if there is one thing that I keep beating the drum for—it's the importance of getting alone and into God's Word. In this work, Sharon creatively paints the cultural picture to help you understand the backdrop of the Gospel of John. She not only points the reader to God's Word but gives a straightforward, simple template, that allows you to carve out and maximize your time in devotions/Bible study. If you are looking for a devotional/Bible study book that is both deep and manageable, this is a wonderful choice!

Pastor Yves Perodin, Jr., Eliot Baptist Church

Sharon's third book offers a great opportunity to discover truth from God's Word and find application for our lives. Using the 4R Method of Bible study, this interactive study of the Gospel of John is simple and easy to follow. Sharon sets the pace through each day of the study allowing each participant space to study and reflect on the passage. Following that, Sharon gives her insights and responses to the Scripture passage. Sharon has included a leader's guide with ample questions for group discussion. As she explains, these questions are not "homework" and there is no pressure to "finish" the questions each week. The purpose of the group study is to help the participants "grow in the understanding of the passage" with insightful questions and application which encourages a deeper understanding of God and His beloved son Jesus.

Lyn Bullock, Board Member, Sweet Selah Ministries

This Bible study has been a huge gift from God and has blessed me beyond what I could have imagined. It is an immersive, relational way to read the Bible and much more of a spiritual conversation with the Lord than a "study" of John. Even more than feeling Loved by Jesus, I am in awe of Him. What a wonderful Savior we have!

Marlene McKenna, Board Member, Sweet Selah Ministries,
Writer/Blogger, havhope.com

Participating in the *Loved* Bible study proved to me that when you step out in faith to meet with God, He does not disappoint. Between the study guide, discussion questions, and feedback from fellow participants, I learned more and more about the character of my Savior and His beloved disciple. I highly recommend *Loved* no matter where you are on your journey in faith.

Anne Alix, Bible Study Test Group Participant

Into the reality of chaotic, difficult, and not-always-understandable daily life comes this blessed study of John, rich in the treasure of His great love, grace, and mercy. Our Savior, Comforter, Provider, and Living Eternal Hope. Truly, there were so many moments as I was reading John and the words of this study that direction, encouragement, reassurance, and hope bounced right into what I was experiencing in life that very day. God is so faithful!

Debbie Briggs

Sharon shares from her heart in *Loved. A Bible Study of the Gospel of John*, and she gets to the heart of John. She draws out biblical and historical facts, so you have a true understanding of the Book of John. You are using the 4R Method so you are active in the learning process yourself and then reading the devotional to further aid in your understanding. A leader's guide is available with insightful questions to aid in making a Bible study for a group. Great for new believers—and seasoned believers too will find nuggets to encourage them in their walk with the Lord.

Julie Munyan

Loved is an excellent Bible study. Sharon has been blessed with a gift and a love to share the truth and depth of God's Word with everyone. She thoroughly accomplished that in Loved. She writes in such a way that the Bible comes alive. I felt like I was right there with the disciples sitting at Jesus' feet while He was teaching them.

Sally Grover

I found the 4R Method encouraging and helpful. Each step made my Bible reading more of a conversation with the Lord than just reading for information. The "R" of "Response" gave me a way to share my thoughts and feelings back to the Lord. Each passage then had a deeper meaning and greater conviction as the Lord and I discussed them together. Sharon's devotional thoughts often added a different perspective to the passage I had not seen. It's nice to listen in to her conversations with the Lord.

Judy Venable

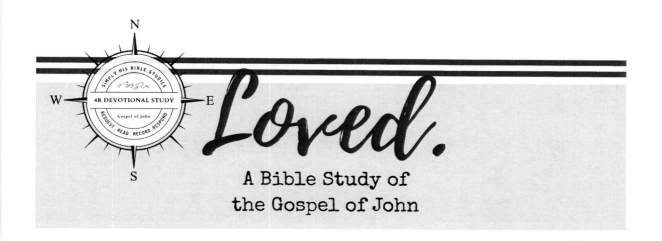

Loved.

A Bible Study of the Gospel of John

SIMPLY HIS BIBLE STUDIES
4R DEVOTIONAL STUDY
Gospel of John
REQUEST · READ · RECORD · RESPOND

SHARON GAMBLE

Harris House Publishing

Loved. A Bible Study of the Gospel of John
Copyright 2022 by Sharon Gamble

Published by Harris House Publishing
harrishousepublishing.com
Colleyville, Texas
USA

Edited by Jan Peck

Cover designed by Kathryn Bailey

Interior designed by Ben Santiago

ISBN: 978-1-946369-62-8

Subject Heading: BIBLE STUDIES / CHRISTIAN LIFE

Printed in the United States of America

Dedicated to

Jan Peck

Long ago and far away, God told you to join me at Sweet Selah Ministries and help me. He knew how much I'd need you not only to correct my overabundant commas, but also to make sure the words I write match the words I meant to write—words that are true and honoring to God and in harmony with His Word. I am so grateful for your partnership with me in this adventure of writing. Yes, I write the books, but you make them so much better. Thank you.

Love you, pal!
Sharon

Forward

by Marlene McKenna

God brought Sharon Gamble into my life in the fall of 2001. She was the national coordinator for a prayer ministry, and I led one of the prayer groups at a small school. When I heard Sharon speak, her passion for God's Word, prayer, and cultivating an intimate relationship with God was obvious. Several years later, I discovered her love for writing, using the same timeless themes. It's no surprise to me that the joy and peace that come from trusting God has spilled over into her books and colored each page. Sharon's writing is winsome and precise, and she has the unique gift of infusing love into every sentence.

James 3:17 defines the heart of her work: "But the wisdom that comes from heaven is first of all pure; then peace-loving, considerate, submissive, full of mercy and good fruit, impartial and sincere" (NIV). All these gifts are reflected in Sharon's books, but especially in the Bible study, *Loved*. Because of this, the Book of John unfolded for me more as a narrative as I absorbed the Scripture reading each day. I saw Jesus as an intimate friend as well as a redeeming Savior.

Prior to *Loved*, I sauntered through daily devotionals and intentionally studied the Bible—*separately*. But, as I read *Loved* and studied the Book of John, my eyes were opened to nuances I had never seen before, like the long conversation Jesus had with His disciples right before His crucifixion. Jesus poured His heart out to His disciples because He loved them and knew the next few days would be heartbreaking, confusing, and even terrifying. In this passage and throughout the study, all the loving, prophetic, intimate, red words just appeared from nowhere and surprised me even though I had read them many times before. What I appreciate most about *Loved* is the way Sharon led us into intimacy with God as we studied the Gospel of John. Then, she transports the truths of John's ancient writing into our everyday, modern lives. This is truly a devotional book that has changed the way I read the Bible and pray.

Fortunately, I had the privilege of leading a small group of women through the *Loved* Bible study. Each of us found it to be different from most studies—more intimate. A foundation was quickly laid for transparency as we shared our lives through our favorite verses and responses to the introspective, yet practical, questions. Moreover, the 4R Method (Request, Read, Record, Respond) creates a predictable cadence that opens the heart to contemplation. It's not only a method but a pattern of conversation.

My prayer is that, after working through this study, you too will know without a doubt that you are deeply loved by God. Hopefully, once you are immersed in *Loved. A Bible Study of the Gospel of John*, you too will be swept away by the all-enveloping love wave of God.

O Lord, you have examined my heart
and know everything about me.
You made all the delicate, inner parts of my body
and knit me together in my mother's womb.
Thank you for making me so wonderfully complex!
Your workmanship is marvelous—how well I know it.
You watched me as I was being formed in utter seclusion,
as I was woven together in the dark of the womb.

You saw me before I was born.
Every day of my life was recorded in your book.
Every moment was laid out
before a single day had passed.

—Psalm 139:1, 13-16

*O*nce, centuries ago, a boy was born to a fisherman and his wife. Nothing set him apart as extraordinary. He had a big brother, James. He was born into a family that fished, so his life was pretty much predetermined. He'd be a fisherman like his dad and someday, along with his brother, manage the fishing firm. Like millions of people born before and after him, he most likely thought he knew what lay before him as he grew up. His name was John, and his life was going to be very different from what he or anyone else would ever have predicted.

John grew up in an uneasy time. On the one hand, Rome had pretty much conquered the known world, so a sort of peace existed, called the Pax Romana. Rome was the victor, so everyone did what Rome said, and, at that time, not too many major wars were going on. Rome built aqueducts and fancy roads so that people could travel more easily between countries in its vast empire. However, peace won at the price of oppression and the sword is a strange sort of peace.

In John's country of Israel, Rome's presence meant that taxes were extraordinarily high and were used by and large to benefit Rome. Despite those roads and aqueducts and such, John's people felt more oppressed than blessed by the way their money was regularly extorted from them and only used to make Rome even greater.

It also meant that John lived in an occupied land. Roman soldiers were a regular sight on the roads. They were in people's business, and they were very determined to keep the peace no matter how violent they needed to be to keep it. John knew all about crucifixion long before Jesus was crucified. It was a horrific specter hanging quite literally over his people, reminding them that Rome would go to any lengths to force them to do the will of Rome.

Let's be clear here. This was not a good time to rock the boat. Most people minded their own business, did their best to pay their taxes and attract no notice from the Romans, and quietly hoped to make it through life poor, but unharmed. It was not a good time to stand out as different. And yet John's life would indeed be different!

The all-wise and all-knowing God ordained that John would be born in the exact same period of time and live in the exact same country where He, as Jesus, chose to be born and live. God took on flesh and dwelled among us for a season. Furthermore, John was one of twelve men chosen by God to be His intimate friends and companions during His sojourn on Earth. John would see impossible sights and hear incredible truths spoken from the very heart of God. He would suffer much. He would be privy to some of Jesus' darkest moments. And yet, He would be loved beyond all reckoning and understanding.

One of John's God-ordained purposes was to write about all he would see and experience during Jesus' three years of active public ministry on Earth. In fact, without John, we would not know the length of time Jesus walked about the country healing and teaching. John alone of the four gospel writers gives us the clues that lead us to believe Jesus actively ministered here for three years. The other gospels do not differentiate between Passovers, but John does. You and I will see this as we walk through his amazing story of life with the Son of God on Earth.

I have named this study very simply. A one-word title: *Loved*. John was bowled over by the love he received from Jesus. He refused to name himself in his gospel, preferring to go by the name he chose for himself: "the disciple whom Jesus loved." Isn't that just the coolest name? It can be your name and mine as well. Our God *so loved the world* John tells us in his most quoted statement in John 3:16. The world is made up of all the people ever born everywhere. So. That includes us. You and me. May we be bowled over and rendered speechless as we read about and comprehend the wide, deep, high, and long love of Christ for His own. That's one of my personal goals for this study, that you walk away knowing you are loved, and, through that knowing, you fulfill the purpose He has for your life.

John had a clearly defined purpose for writing the Gospel of John. As we finish this introduction, let's ponder the two verses that declare his intentions. They're found at the very end of his gospel, and I find them so incredibly helpful. We don't have to guess at all why he wrote this book. He tells us:

> *The disciples saw Jesus do many other miraculous signs in addition to the ones recorded in this book. But these are written so that you may continue to believe that Jesus is the Messiah, the Son of God, and that by believing in him you will have life by the power of his name.* — John 20:30-31

Don't you love that John wants you, the reader, to believe Jesus is the Messiah, the Son of God, and that by believing you will have life by the power of His Name? Guess what? John also loves you. His heart is for you to know Jesus, John's dear and best Friend. Are you ready? Let's pack up our Bibles, journals, pens, and listening hearts and learn together as we enter this Bible study. *You are loved.*

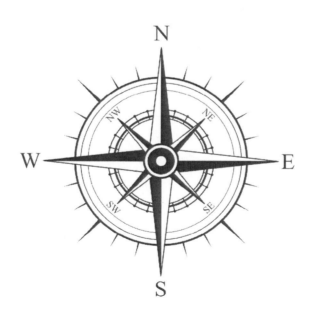

*L*oved is an interactive Bible study. This means that you and I are going to examine the Gospel of John together. It's a nine-week study with five lessons each week. (On the other two days, consider reading a Psalm or a chapter of Proverbs to keep your everyday quiet time habit.) I'm very excited to "be with you" as you dig into God's Word. I hope you will feel free to email me at any time, letting me know what God is teaching you. You can reach me at sharon@sweetselah.org.

Jesus tells us clearly what our daily priority should be. When He was asked which is the greatest commandment, here was His response: *"Jesus replied: 'Love the Lord your God with all your heart and with all your soul and with all your mind.' This is the first and greatest commandment"* (Matthew 22:37-38 NIV). Always, always . . . God gets first place in our hearts and lives. You are most likely a busy person, and some days are going to be crammed full of activities. Your set-apart time to spend with the Lord may be short, but that's exactly why I recommend giving God and His Word the first minutes of your day. It's the best way to keep the importance of time with Him at the very top of your "to do" list. And what *joy* you will find in meeting with Him. Quite frankly, it is my favorite part of the day.

This study begins each day with just you and God alone. I'll lead you in a prayer each morning to focus our hearts on the Lord so that we may be receptive to His words to us. Then, you'll do your own quiet study with Him. You'll easily be able to follow the directions. After that, we'll "talk" about it. My commentary is meant to be read *after* you and the Lord have spent precious time together. *He* is to be our first love; let's always give Him first place.

John 1:1-18

Request: Dear Father, as I start this study, please help me to be a faithful learner. Open my eyes and reveal to me new truths that will help me love You more and live more lovingly. In Jesus' Name, Amen.

Read: John 1:1-18

Record: Write down one verse from this passage that stood out to you.

Respond: Write a short prayer, talking to God about that verse.

I have always loved this portion of God's Word. It's hard to read without tears in my eyes. John does not start with a tale about himself and how he found Jesus or even how Jesus found him. John starts at the very, very beginning, echoing the first verse in the entire Bible: *"In the beginning God created the heavens and the earth"* (Genesis 1:1). John starts . . . with God. He gives first place to Jesus, the Word, God made flesh, who came and dwelled among us. How beautifully John illustrates that first commandment to love God most of all.

The amount of theology in these first eighteen verses of John is astounding. I think one could spend a lifetime reading and meditating on these verses and never run out of insights and new understandings about our amazing God. One God, showing Himself to us in three persons, one of whom is the focus of this gospel: Jesus Christ, Son of God, Messiah, God-in-flesh.

One of the primary messages John is drilling into our heads is that Jesus is indeed God. He didn't "start" in Mary's womb. He existed before the creation of the world; in fact, He created the world! The mystery of the Trinity is right here in these verses. God is so big and so vast and so unlike us that He has three persons within One Being. He is one Person "seen" by us in three distinct ways: Father,  Son, and Holy Spirit. No one can ever fathom the mystery of the Trinity—or the mystery of God's deep love for us or a million other things about God that are too deep for us. But John helps us see the complexity and marvel at it in these verses. Before Jesus was born as a human, He already existed. He is God. He always was and always will be. John wastes no time at all in laying that out for us.

Another big message for us is that God chose to "dwell among us" for a season. God, the Son, distilled Himself into a tiny zygote, a microscopic embryo, and took the journey all of us take from conception to death, feeling what we felt, inhabiting the limits of a human body, feeling the weight of time and gravity, and experiencing emotions as we do. It is a stunning thing for God to do. He didn't have to limit Himself in this way, but He wanted to for the salvation of our souls.

John also captures for us the huge sadness and irony involved in this taking on of flesh. People rejected Him. He created them. They only breathed because He held the world together, which is still true of us today. And yet "the world didn't recognize him" (v. 10). We shake our heads in dismay as we think of the humility and self-restraint of the God who walked among us and endured such disregard without striking back as we deserved. We secretly wonder if *we* would have acknowledged Him as Messiah or if we would have ignored Him. This time on Earth when Jesus took on flesh and walked among us? It wasn't easy. Not at all.

The last thing I want us to notice today is that John starts to show us a hint of why he is writing this gospel. Scholars believe that the other three gospels had already been written before John's. Matthew, Mark, and Luke recorded tons of incidents and stories of Jesus' life from His birth through His public ministry, His death and resurrection to ascension. John's gospel is very different from those three. They share a lot of the same stories with fun, differing details that flesh out each miracle and event for us, but, by and large, John's mission is to tell what they did not. He speaks more of *who* Jesus claimed to be and shares more words Jesus spoke privately to His disciples. He fills in a lot of gaps. And John was there. I can almost hear the awe in his heart when he writes, "...And we have seen his glory, the glory of the Father's one and only Son" (v. 14). John saw all this! With his own eyes. He had the immense privilege—and responsibility—of walking with the Son of God. And John saw His glory. As we read his book, we are going to stand in awe with John, marveling at the glory of God through Jesus. I'm so pumped by this concept. We have the privilege of reading an eyewitness account by one of Jesus' best friends, written later in his life as a mature follower of Christ, faithful to the end. Buckle up. It's going to be quite the ride.

My verse: "For the law was given through Moses, but God's unfailing love and faithfulness came through Jesus Christ" (John 1:17).

My response: Dear Lord, over and over in the New Testament, You remind me that the law was a teacher that showed Your people their need of a Savior. How grateful I am that through Your sacrificial death and victorious resurrection, I am free from the burden of living under the law, never measuring up, and always having to give another sacrifice as the Israelites had to do. Instead, I live in relationship with You, serving with the help of the Spirit, and being forgiven over and over through Your grace. Thank You for Your unfailing love and faithfulness to me, Your child. I am loved. You whisper that to me over and over in this very first section of John. You made me, Lord Jesus. You gave me the rights of a child of the King of kings through Your death and resurrection—and through Your life on Earth, Your unfailing love and faithfulness are revealed. Thank You.

John 1:19-34

Request: Dear Heavenly Father, thank You for giving us Jesus. As I continue to read today, give me insight, Lord. What would You teach me? How would You prepare me for the day ahead? You alone know what I will face. Give me a listening heart. In Jesus' Name, Amen.

Read: John 1:19-34

Record: Write down one verse from this passage that stood out to you.

Respond: Write a short prayer, talking to God about that verse.

_____

_____

_____

_____

_____

_____

_____

*I*n today's session, it becomes apparent that John has changed his focus. The first verses in his gospel gave us an overarching look at who Jesus is. John stated big, theological truths for us and made sure we knew from the very beginning that Jesus was God come to Earth.

Now begins John's story. He doesn't start at Jesus' birth or conception like Matthew and Luke did. He starts with the very first announcement that Jesus was Messiah. In this passage, we meet another guy named John. It's a common name, and since this is a true story, no one is making up new names just to keep us from being confused as one might in a novel. Nope. Two Johns figured large in Jesus' life.

John the Baptist first recognized Jesus while they were both still tiny babies in their mothers' wombs! John's purpose from before he was born was to herald the arrival of the Messiah. Let's just pause for a moment here. God makes people on purpose for a purpose. Yeah, I know not all of us are given visible and sometimes scary purposes like John the Baptist and the disciples and the prophets. That doesn't mean, however, that God hasn't wired you and me with purpose, too. I hope that as we read and as you seek Him in these pages, you will grow an increased awareness of God's good purposes for you, dear one.

I love how John the Baptist is not interested in being the main man at all. He's really clear in this passage that it's not about him. His job is to point out the Messiah to the people of his time and to prepare them for Jesus' arrival. John the Baptist preaches a lot on repentance. He points out sins quite bluntly and forcefully. You see, we are all full of embarrassingly evil thoughts and intentions. We try to hide them and keep a shiny veneer on display for the world, but I don't think there's a person on this planet who would love to have their every thought and attitude broadcast live for the world to see, let alone some of their actions and deeds. I know I wouldn't!

We all need help. We all have issues. John the Baptist's job was to help people realize this and not excuse themselves. Then, he baptized them, washing them figuratively "clean" and signifying to them they could have a fresh start.

His baptism was limited, of course. Without Jesus' saving work on the cross, the people "washed clean" were unable to stay that way, but they were made aware that they needed saving. Our John makes it very clear that John the Baptist emphatically testified that Jesus was indeed Messiah and Savior. Aren't you just blown away by verse 27? Reading in the New Living Translation, I was struck by John the Baptist's humility and awe of Jesus. Here's what he said: *"Though his ministry follows mine, I'm not even worthy to be his slave and untie the straps of his sandal."* Whoa. Now that's humility. Basically, to be Jesus' slave or to even touch His feet would be an honor far too great for John the Baptist. That's how *big* Jesus is, and John the Baptist has no desire to eclipse him. His desire was for us to know that Jesus was Messiah. Our two Johns have a lot in common, don't they?

My verse: "He is the one I was talking about when I said, 'A man is coming after me who is far greater than I am, for he existed long before me'" (John 1:30).

My response: As Your forerunner, John the Baptist was given great knowledge. He knew that You were the Lamb, the sacrifice (v. 29), that You existed before Your human birth (v. 30). What wondrous and impossible certainties! And here is John the Baptist, right at the beginning, Lord Jesus, declaring Your uniqueness, echoing John the disciple, who wrote this gospel. Lord, I love these echoes that repeat the truths You want me to know and believe.

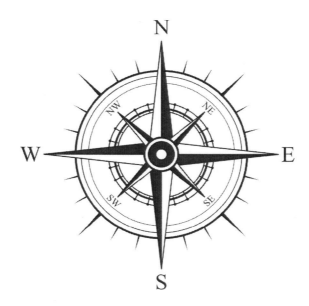

John 1:35-51

Request: Oh, faithful God, thank You for this new day. Help me to follow You closely in all I say and do. And, Lord, as I sit here now and read Your Living Word to me, help it to resonate. Enable me to truly grasp the truths You have for me. In Jesus' Name, Amen.

Read: John 1:35-51

Record: Write down one verse from this passage that stood out to you.

Respond: Write a short prayer, talking to God about that verse.

_____

_____

_____

_____

_____

_____

_____

_____

*I*n this portion of Scripture, John gives a very abbreviated version of Jesus gathering His first disciples. No mention is made of Jesus calling them from their fishing boats. At first, they just "hung out" with Jesus. Later, would come that more formal calling when Jesus said, "Follow me," and they left everything to follow Him. I love that we are given a glimpse of some earlier and different stories of the disciples' first meetings with Jesus. Did you notice something subtle about the two disciples of John the Baptist? He had been preparing the way for Messiah, and these two realized that Messiah had come! They simply left John the Baptist and began following Jesus. Our John in his gospel only names one of them, Andrew. And yet, John knew exactly what happened that day. Is it possible the other disciple with Andrew was actually . . . John?

In the days ahead, we will see that John refuses to bring any attention to himself. His favorite name in referring to himself is "the disciple whom Jesus loved." So, I'm just pondering here. Perhaps John was a part-time follower of John the Baptist as well as a fisherman. I love that John the Baptist's job was never to gather and keep followers. His job was always to point them to Jesus. We would do well to remember that in our own lives. Our jobs, too, are to point people to Jesus.

In this short passage, we glimpse Jesus' fondness for these men as unique individuals. In Andrew's brother, Simon, later renamed Peter, Jesus sees a man who will one day become . . . a rock, a solid man of faith capable of leading the early church. I picture Jesus smiling at Nathaniel's bluntness and

initial distrust. Jesus sees the pure heart behind the bluster, a heart that seeks what is right and true, and He lets Nathaniel know how He values integrity. Jesus quickly points out exactly where Nathaniel had been sitting when his friend Philip approached him. This knowledge could not have been known to Jesus except by supernatural means, and Nathaniel, convinced by this miraculous tidbit, declares that Jesus is the Son of God.

Did you notice? In every portion of chapter one that we have read this week, someone is stating for us that Jesus is the Son of God, Messiah. John is leaving no stone unturned. The message is clear. We are not talking about some very nice man who preached cool sermons. We are talking about God. Deity. A miraculous, one-time happening when God walked on Earth in human skin like ours. Jesus is front and center in John's thoughts and writings. I want so much for that to be true of me. I want people to hear me speak more of Him and less of me. And I surely have a lot of growing to do in this area. How about you?

My verse: "Then he said, 'I tell you the truth, you will all see heaven open and the angels of God going up and down on the Son of Man, the one who is the stairway between heaven and earth'" (John 1:51).

My response: Jesus looks at this unlikely crew assembled from obscure villages, working men, rough about the edges, and tells them they will see astounding sights. I love this translation, Lord. The thought that You, Lord Jesus, are the stairway between us earthlings and Heaven. You came to give us Heaven, and I am sure that when I do finally see it, I'll be more overwhelmed than I can even imagine. That You are preparing such an incredible place to be my forever home . . . amazing, miraculous, indescribable. Thank You.

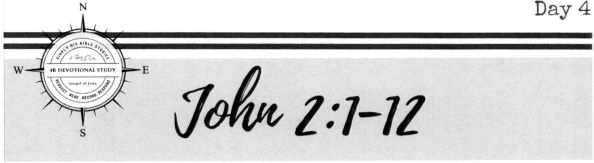

Request: Thank You, Father-God, for sending Your Son to us. Help me to see Jesus with fresh eyes, learning and growing closer to Him as I study. I need Your help, Lord. I am not able to see spiritual truths without Your help. Please be near me as I read. In Jesus' Name, Amen.

Read: John 2:1-12

Record: Write down one verse from this passage that stood out to you.

Respond: Write a short prayer, talking to God about that verse.

*T*oday, we had the privilege of witnessing a miracle through John's eyes. In that culture, running out of wine at one's own daughter's wedding would have been more than a bit embarrassing; it would have shamed the parents of the bride before all their family and friends. It's still not acceptable to throw a wedding feast and run out of food or drink, is it? Can you imagine going to a reception and some of the guests have nothing to drink? Or maybe eat? Humiliating in any culture. So, I love that Jesus' mother Mary noticed and brought it to her Son's attention.

I also love her response to His quizzical comment that His time had not yet come. Mary lets it be. She doesn't argue with Him at all or try to convince Him to help. She simply tells the servants to do whatever Jesus says. And perhaps Jesus would say they should do nothing, right? How did Mary know what Jesus would do? Luke's gospel tells us that when an angel brought the news to Mary that she would be the mother of the Messiah, other than asking how that could possibly be, she simply responded that she was the Lord's servant willing to do whatever He asked. Mary trusted God. And she demonstrates that in this passage as well. She states the need, and then she rests.

I tend not to do that. I tend to state and restate the need. I tend to come up with all kinds of solutions and ideas for how God should "fix" whatever I believe needs fixing. I want to bring my needs before Him in quieter ways, telling Him my troubles and laying them at His feet, knowing He has heard, and He will answer as is best.

As we saw in the reading, Jesus chose to turn water into wine. He chose to publicly perform a miracle that would by its very nature catapult Him and His disciples into the limelight. Don't you just love that His first miracle was at a wedding? Did you know that we, His people, are often referred to as His bride? It's true! He loves us so deeply, so irrevocably, once we come to Him, that He equates it to the forever covenantal relationship of marriage. Savor these verses and marvel at God's deep, deep love for you:

*For your Creator will be your husband; the L*ORD *of Heaven's Armies is his name! He is your Redeemer, the Holy One of Israel, the God of all the earth.* —Isaiah 54:5

Your children will commit themselves to you, O Jerusalem, just as a young man commits himself to his bride. Then God will rejoice over you as a bridegroom rejoices over his bride. —Isaiah 62:5

For husbands, this means love your wives, just as Christ loved the church. He gave up his life for her to make her holy and clean, washed by the cleansing of God's word. —Ephesians 5:25-26

"Let us be glad and rejoice, and let us give honor to him. For the time has come for the wedding feast of the Lamb, and his bride has prepared herself. She has been given the finest of pure white linen to wear." For the fine linen represents the good deeds of God's holy people. And the angel said to me, "Write this: Blessed are those who are invited to the wedding feast of the Lamb." And he added, "These are true words that come from God." —Revelation 19:7-9

One final little thought for today. Sometimes we think of God as being very stern and strict and not smiling very much. This would be false. Jesus, God in the flesh, went to a wedding feast with His friends! He enjoyed celebrations. Our God brings love, joy, and peace to us. It's a happy thing to be His.

My verse: "He said, 'Now dip some out, and take it to the master of ceremonies.' So the servants followed his instructions" (John 2:8).

My response: With what authority and confidence You must have spoken, Lord! What You asked made no practical sense. Dip out water and deliver it to the guy in charge? Yet, they obeyed. I love that. Help me to be as willing to obey unlikely commands from You.

John 2:13-25

Request: Thank You, Father, for this carved-out space of time I have to simply sit with You. Keep me from the distractions of my phone and the endless to-do list in my head. This is Your time, Lord. I wait to hear from You as I open Your Word. Please speak to me. In Jesus' Name, Amen.

Read: John 2:13-25

Record: Write down one verse from this passage that stood out to you.

Respond: Write a short prayer, talking to God about that verse.

*T*oday, we've come to a very different kind of event, haven't we? Yesterday, we saw Jesus celebrating at a wedding. Today, we see Him quite thoroughly clearing out the Temple. Wow. The gospel writers over and over say that Jesus "spoke with authority." I guess He did! No one tried to stop Him. They were too busy jumping out of His way! It wasn't like He turned over a table and then was stopped. Nope. My New Living Translation puts it this way: "Jesus made a whip from some ropes and chased them all out of the Temple ..." (v. 15). I can't even imagine the shock and dismay on people's faces as they watched this vehement rebuke of those who had turned a place of worship into a marketplace where poor people could be extorted as they came to bring their sacrifices to God. It was appalling. And Jesus dealt with it.

When the Jewish leaders questioned Jesus about His authority, they demanded a sign. Jesus' reply made no sense at the time: "Destroy this temple and three days later, I will have it standing again" (v.19). That's an intriguing statement and would have "stuck" in puzzled minds. Not until after He was crucified and on the third day rose again did the disciples have an "aha!" moment when they saw Jesus' words, spoken way back at the beginning of His ministry, come true absolutely. Jesus was God in flesh. He was, in a sense, the "temple" where God resided. What an amazing concept to ponder.

What do we learn about Jesus from this incident? We certainly discover that, although He was full of love and mercy, He was also angry at injustice and was willing to do something about it. At times, we tend to want to make Jesus in "our" image. If we have gentle personalities, we love talking about His kindness and mercy. If we are more justice-oriented folks, we may get all fired up when we see Him clearing out the Temple and putting those unscrupulous men in their place. Where do you fall on this spectrum?

If you are on the gentle side, please be assured that Jesus was and is a gentle, loving Savior, whose heart is for His people. He leaves the 99 sheep in the fold to go hike the mountains and bring back that one stray little lamb. He forgives sin and welcomes those who are not wanted in society into His fold, not willing that any should perish. He told us the two greatest commands are to love God and love others. He went even further and urged us to not only love our enemies but to pray for them.

If you are on the justice side, rejoice that your God sees and is angered by injustice. His fiercest rebukes were saved for those who faked their faith. Whether they were the Pharisees, who loved the rules but not the God who made them, or whether they were the money-changers, who cared only for their profits and nothing for the sacredness of sacrifice in the Temple. But, in His Kingdom, He shows no favorites. He wants Jew and Greek, male and female, slave and free to all know that they are equally His: "There is neither Jew nor Gentile, neither slave nor free, nor is there male and female, for you are all one in Christ Jesus" (Galatians 3:28 NIV). He sees oppression, and He is angered by it. Someday, all manner of things will be set to rights. You can count on it. It's why we should earnestly pray for our enemies who have not turned to Him. Their fate is appalling if they don't look to Him for rescue.

My verse: "'All right,' Jesus replied. 'Destroy this temple, and in three days I will raise it up'" (John 2:19).

My response: Jesus—at the very beginning of Your public ministry—first Passover—You already knew Your death was coming. You called Your body a temple, and it was and is. Your earthly body housed God. It's so amazing to me, Lord, that Your Spirit now resides in every believer. My body is also a temple, housing You, Living God! (1 Corinthians 6:19).

*"He must become greater and greater, and
I must become less and less."*

— JOHN 3:30 —

WEEK TWO

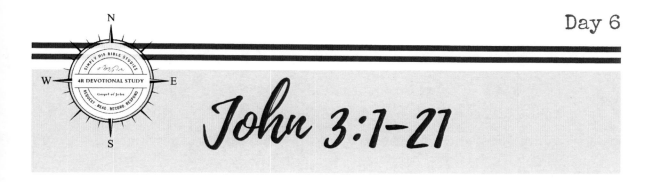

John 3:1-21

Request: Heavenly Father, thank You for this little space of time for just You and me to meet. Help me as I read this Word that You have "God-breathed" for me and countless others, help me to read with awe and a growing awareness that You speak through it. In Jesus' Name, Amen.

Read: John 3:1-21

Record: Write down one verse from this passage that stood out to you.

Respond: Write a short prayer, talking to God about that verse.

_____

_____

_____

_____

_____

_____

_____

We've come now to the most famous and widely quoted verse in the Bible. But before we get to John 3:16, let's take a look at the man who first heard these words from Jesus' own mouth. Nicodemus. I love that Nicodemus was both a Pharisee and a member of the Sanhedrin. As human beings, we tend to lump people into categories. We decide that all the people, who believe differently than we do on some hot political issue, are evil and have terrible motives. We instantly dislike those who root against our favorite team. This is not right. God looks at the heart of a person, and sometimes someone who appears to be on the wrong side is actually trying hard to do right. This would be Nicodemus. Unlike many of his fellow Pharisees, who were set in their ways and refused to question them, Nicodemus noted  Jesus' miracles and reasoned that only God could do such things. He didn't understand Jesus, but he didn't close off his heart from hearing what Jesus had to say. And what Jesus had to say to Nicodemus was huge.

Nicodemus started with a polite comment about how he saw God working through Jesus in the miracles. But Jesus didn't want to waste a minute of this secret meeting on pleasantries. So, He immediately changed the subject to what mattered most. He had come to Earth to give people spiritual life. Just as we have a physical birth, we are invited to be "born again" spiritually. Our first birth happened without our knowledge or consent, didn't it? But this spiritual awakening and birth? That's up to us. God graciously offers us new life in Him that will last forever. Do we completely understand this? Nope. No more than we understand why the wind blows in one direction and then another. But it does blow and as it does, change happens to the surroundings. When we receive what God offers, we are swept into a new way of living, and change happens to our surroundings too. It's wonderful!

John packs so much truth into this one sentence, words he remembers through the Holy Spirit as he writes, words that Jesus spoke to Nicodemus: "For God so loved the world that He gave His only begotten Son, that whoever believes in Him should not perish but have everlasting life" (John 3:16 NKJV). How do you and I know we are loved? God loved us so much that He sent His Son to die for us so that we can live forever. You and me? We are deeply, sacrificially *loved*. We often miss the impact of the verse that immediately follows, but it's super important too. It was especially important for our Pharisee to hear. "For God did not send His Son into the world to condemn the world, but that the world through Him might be saved" (John 3:17 NKJV).

Pharisees were really, really big on following all the rules. Even teensy tiny ones about how exactly to wash your hands and for how long. They thought their righteousness was wrapped up in ceremony and outward obedience to a very long list of rules and commands. But they were wrong. They were quite "judgy" about those who did not keep the rules as well as they did. I think maybe we all tend to be the most judgmental when others can't do what we find easy. And yet, Jesus follows this beautiful verse on God's love with an explanation. He came to save and not condemn. Righteousness is found through His saving of us and not through endless keeping of rules. We will watch John repeatedly drive that message home in the weeks ahead. For now, let's simply be amazed that God came in the form of Jesus the "only begotten Son" to save because He so loved you. And me. And the world.

My verse: "No one has ever gone to heaven and returned. But the Son of Man has come down from heaven" (John 3:13).

My response: Lord Jesus, I can't even imagine the contrast between Heaven and earth. You knew because You had lived in Heaven and were now inhabiting human flesh on our broken planet. Thank You for that huge sacrifice—to leave the glorious lightness and joy of Heaven for us. I'm astounded and grateful just thinking about it this morning.

John 3:22-36

Request: Dear Lord Jesus, thank You that You so loved me that You came to Earth to save me and not condemn me as I fully deserve. Help me to focus on Your Word today. Show me the verse that You want me to treasure in my heart as I go about the day's tasks. In Your Name, I ask this. Amen.

Read: John 3:22-36

Record: Write down one verse from this passage that stood out to you.

Respond: Write a short prayer, talking to God about that verse.

_____

_____

_____

_____

_____

_____

_____

We are blessed today with yet another glimpse of John the Baptist's great humility. As Jesus' fame grows, more and more people are flocking to Him. After all, John the Baptist is limited to rousing sermons convicting people of their evil ways and then baptizing. Jesus is healing the sick, restoring sight to the blind, and also speaking ardently to crowds. And His disciples are also baptizing. Suddenly, Jesus is more appealing to the masses. Does this trouble John? Is his waning popularity bothering him? Not at all. He's always known his role, and he is happy in it. His job has been to prepare hearts for Jesus' message and eventual salvation. He wants people to follow Jesus. His greatest success is to see the people turn to Messiah. I love his simple sentence about Jesus, "He must become greater and greater, and I must become less and less" (v. 30).

This needs to be our goal as well. Once we are saved and brought into God's Kingdom as His children, we are left here on Earth for one huge purpose: To shine the light He has given us by the way we live so that others might also choose Him. Like John the Baptist, we are to point to Jesus. Our greatest joy should be when someone sees our first love, Jesus, and begins to love Him too. After we attain Heaven, let's be remembered as ones who pointed others to the God who loves them and died for them!

I was super intrigued by John 3:34. John helps us develop our understanding of God throughout this great gospel. Here in one verse, we see the concept of a triune God: "For he is sent by God. He speaks God's words, for God gives him the Spirit without limit." Jesus is not only sent by God, He speaks God's words. And that  is because He is not only **with** God, He **is** God in human form. In addition, He has the Spirit within Him without limit. It reminds me of the wind illustration we read about yesterday. We know wind exists, but don't ask us to explain it fully. God is One being in three distinct persons.

We know this from the Bible, but don't ask us to explain it fully. After all, how does a finite human being ever fully explain an all-powerful God?

Let's walk away from this passage today in awe of this God who came to Earth and felt what we feel. This God who healed people and touched them with His words and His power. This God who loved us enough to die for us. May He become greater and greater as we point to Him through our daily lives.

My verse: "It is the bridegroom who marries the bride, and the bridegroom's friend is simply glad to stand with him and hear his vows. Therefore I am filled with joy at his success" (John 3:29).

My response: I love that You are our Bridegroom, and we—Your church—are Your bride! Give me John's attitude, Lord, to always point to You and to simply be glad to be the "bridegroom's friend," who introduces You to others, and then someday, as part of the church, to be Your bride.

John 4:1-26

Request: Slow me down, Lord, please. Still my anxious, busy heart so that I can truly be all here with You, eager to listen and learn. Teach me, please, as I read and study. In Jesus' Name, Amen.

Read: John 4:1-26

Record: Write down one verse from this passage that stood out to you.

Respond: Write a short prayer, talking to God about that verse.

*O*h, I do love the story of the Samaritan woman at the well. John chooses his stories well. He tells fewer stories overall than the other three gospel writers, but the ones he includes are for very specific reasons. Each one tells us more about who Jesus is and who He claimed to be. This one is so fun because Jesus singles out an outcast of huge magnitude as the very first person to hear Him declare that He is Messiah. Isn't that cool? He didn't march into Herod's palace and tell the king. He didn't ride off to Rome to tell the emperor. He didn't request an audience with the Sanhedrin to make an announcement to them. He didn't even tell His disciples first straight out. Nope. He chose a shunned woman from a shunned part of Israel. This should clearly underline for us that Jesus has come for the least among us. We just saw Him spend time with Nicodemus, one of the "greats" of his time. Now we see Jesus with one of the "leasts."

Where do you fall on this spectrum? Were you raised in a Christian home, child of a godly pastor, perhaps, and well-versed in Scripture since your youth? *He wants you and He loves you.* Are you more like the Samaritan woman who had failed marriages and was not living a sin-free life at all, shunned by "respectable folk"? *He wants you and He loves you.* He came not to condemn but to save. We learned that a couple of days ago, and now we are seeing it lived out in action as He talks with this favored lady.

I love how Jesus used a commonplace need, thirst, to launch a spiritual discussion. I love how He started with humility. He needed help. He could not reach the water in the well without a bucket, and this dearly loved Samaritan woman had the bucket. He didn't swoop down on her, all high and mighty. He asked for help. You know, if we want to reach people for Christ ourselves, we also need to be humble. It's okay to admit we have needs. Our job isn't to somehow show that because we are Christians, we are sailing through life easily

without any troubles. Nope. Our job is to show that despite troubles, despite our flaws, we are loved by the one true God. Deeply and utterly. He must be the One who looks good. Not us!

He also treated this woman with respect. When she wanted to discuss the theological disagreement over which mountain was the correct one for worship, He engaged her and didn't shut her down. Of course, He also spoke of new truths to her and opened up a whole new way of worship to her—in spirit and in truth—not by rules and laws. He made a statement that still resonates in my heart today. "But those who drink the water I give will never be thirsty again. It becomes a fresh, bubbling spring within them, giving them eternal life" (v. 14). What a beautiful gift He has given us! His Spirit now resides within us, energizing and strengthening us from the inside out and preparing us for the day when we step into everlasting life with Him! Wow. Wow. Wow. This is the very good news God asks us to share. And in this passage, Jesus models so well for us how it's done.

My verse: "Jesus replied, 'If you only knew the gift God has for you and who you are speaking to, you would ask me, and I would give you living water'" (John 4:10).

My response: *That phrase, "if you only knew" resonates. Lord, help me to see those spiritual truths that would help me live in light of eternity. Help me to pant for living water and for You, eternal God. There's so much I still don't see and know. Teach me, Lord. Fill me with living, life-giving water straight from You.*

John 4:27-42

Request: Dear Father, thank You for being my living water and strengthening me from within. I come to You today thirsty. Please teach me and fill me fully as I look to You and what You have for me in Your Word. In Jesus' Name, Amen.

Read: John 4:27-42

Record: Write down one verse from this passage that stood out to you.

Respond: Write a short prayer, talking to God about that verse.

$\mathcal{T}$oday, we finished the story of Jesus and the Samaritan woman and also looked at the results of her acceptance of Him as Messiah. John tells this story slowly and in great detail. It's important, and that's why we are taking two full days to ponder it. We left off with Jesus' startling proclamation to the woman at the well that He, Himself, is Messiah. She believes Him. Why? Well, there is that little matter of Him having never met her before in His life and yet knowing the intimate details of her personal life. How could He possibly have known she'd had five husbands and was now living with a man who wasn't even her husband? Just like our Nathaniel, who was stunned that Jesus had seen him under a fig tree when clearly, He . . . *hadn't*. This woman's jaw must have dropped when Jesus calmly stated the facts.

Notice that He didn't give her a lecture about her dubious marital record. One of my greatest regrets as a parent was that, when our girls had done wrong, I tended to lecture them waaaay more than was necessary or advisable. They knew what they had done wasn't right. The lecture only ground away their sense of feeling loved and cherished. Jesus didn't need to tell this lady that five marriages plus a live-in  situation were wrong. He just stated the facts. She knew it and lived with the shame and guilt that Satan loves to beat us down with over and over. Jesus knew what she needed and what she didn't need. (*Father, give me wisdom like Jesus had to not belabor someone else's sins to them in ways that hurt and don't help!*)

I suspect another reason the woman believed was Jesus Himself. His confidence in His declaration, combined with His loving heart open to this woman in gentleness, would have been undeniable for one who had eyes to see. And God had clearly ordained that this would be the day this broken woman would finally see that she was loved.

So, as the disciples stand there in awkward, horrified silence, she runs back to the village and without shame or timidity starts telling everyone she's met the Messiah! The disciples, meanwhile, are sort of focused on the food. They were probably all hungry after the walk and jaunt into town, so they return to the task they'd been given and urge Jesus to eat. However, Jesus is too energized and thrilled at this converted woman's joy to even focus on food. Can you just see it? Food? They want Him to eat when what has just happened was a life change that affected a broken person's eternity? He's all about doing His Father's will. This excursion to the well was obviously God-directed from the beginning, and Jesus is rejoicing—just like He does today when someone far from Him comes near and discovers that they too are loved.

My verse: "Then Jesus explained: 'My nourishment comes from doing the will of God, who sent me, and from finishing his work'" (John 4:34).

My response: Your great joy and delight was seeing lost souls redeemed. What was food compared to that? Lord, You came to seek and to save those who were lost and helpless without You. Your heart is for us. This verse speaks tenderly to me. You love it when we enter Your Kingdom! Thank You for being my Rescuer and Redeemer.

John 4:43-54

Request: As I sit here this morning, Lord, please clear my mind of all distractions. Enable me to focus on Your words. Show me my verse and teach me how to live well today. In Jesus' Name, Amen.

Read: John 4:43-54

Record: Write down one verse from this passage that stood out to you.

Respond: Write a short prayer, talking to God about that verse.

*W*e finish up this chapter reading about an encounter with a "government official." Isn't it interesting that John has taken us from an important member of the Jewish religious community (Nicodemus) to a woman with no social standing (our woman at the well) to a governing official? I love this! We see in one small chapter of this book that *God so loved the world.* This government official is in great distress. You know, no matter how wealthy and powerful we are, we are not invincible. We can die in an earthquake. We can fall and break our legs. Our children can still get sick and die. This broken, fallen world we live in has troubles aplenty. And those troubles hit us all. Rich and poor, famous and anonymous alike.

This man is naturally worried sick about his son, who has a burning fever. He is dying. Jesus was in Cana again, where His first miracle of turning water into wine took place. The official came from Capernaum, a town about 20 miles away. Since Capernaum was a lake town, the journey to Cana at a higher elevation was uphill all the way. This was not a simple stroll at all. Our official was desperate. Can you imagine how he must have begged with weakened limbs and breathlessness, pleading with Jesus to come and help his dying son? The journey itself tells us both the desperation of the situation and the dedication of the father.

Jesus first asks an enigmatic question before He heals this boy. "Will you never believe in me unless you see miraculous signs and wonders?" (v. 48). This is a question we need to ask ourselves. Because guess what? Miracles are rare and don't always happen just because we ask. God is still in the miracle business . . . crazy, unexplainable healings take place as we pray, and money we need to pay bills shows up just in time. I have several little journals I keep of the miracles I have seen from God's good hand, and I have seen an abundance of unexplained blessings. Praise God! *But miracles are not to be had on demand.* Not everyone I prayed would live . . . has lived. I have asked God to heal me from Meniere's Disease. He has not. (At least not yet!) You've seen that too. We ask in faith, believing, and sometimes we don't receive what we asked for. That's reality.

So, here's the question. Will we only believe God is real and God is good if He always does what we ask? If that were the case, what would that make God? Would He be in charge of running the universe . . . or would we? Who knows more about the future and what is best in the long run? God . . . or us? We need to settle in our souls that God is God—and we are not—and He is good and per-fect in all His ways. When terrible things happen, and they do, these facts about God do not change. Do we always understand? No. Are we thrilled when He chooses not to answer the way we asked? Um. Definitely no. I've cried out to God in agony as I watched a loved one lose her sixth child to miscarriage . . . *why??* But I always come back to the belief that He is God, and He is good, and someday He will help me understand if that is necessary. My belief in God cannot be based on whether or not He chooses to give me everything I want. That's way too subjective. He either is or isn't, regardless of my personal trials. And I would rather go through a trial with Him, knowing He never leaves me, than walk away in a huff and feel the emptiness that would come without His dear and loving Presence. How about you?

Back to our government official. Jesus simply states the boy will live. He must have said it with superb confidence (as well He ought since He knew the truth of it) because the father believed, turned around, and went back home. What sealed the deal for this father and his whole household, though, was when they discovered that the exact moment the fever left was that moment when Jesus declared the boy well. Now that's supernatural power. There was no touching the forehead or giving a special drink or breathing life into the boy. Nope. Jesus was about 20 miles away. But God was right there with this man's son and, in His mercy, healed him. Oh, what a God we serve!

You know what? Even though my Father sometimes tells me "no" when I ask, I'm going to keep asking Him. Because often, He says "yes"! I believe He has the power to raise people from the dead. And so I will ask and then trust that He does know best, even if the answer is not to my liking.

My verse: "Then Jesus told him, 'Go back home. Your son will live!' And the man believed what Jesus said and started home" (John 4:50).

My response: Just like that. Lord Jesus, I love how this boy was healed while You were miles away! For somehow, although You were God in flesh, God was not contained just in Your body. God as Spirit healed. This is a mystery to me, but it's such a comfort. I can pray for loved ones far away from me and know You are right there with them. My prayers can yield Your touch when I am too far away to touch. Thank You.

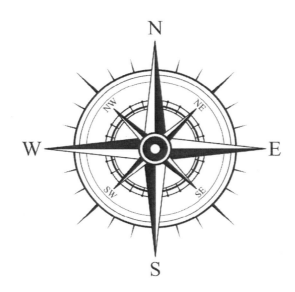

Jesus replied, "I am the bread of life. Whoever comes to me will never be hungry again. Whoever believes in me will never be thirsty."

— JOHN 6:35 —

WEEK THREE

John 5:1-15

Request: Heavenly Father, teach me from the words I will read today in Your Word. Open my eyes to see why they were written and what You want me to learn. Lord, I need You as I read. I welcome You, Holy Spirit, in these quiet moments. In Jesus' Name, Amen.

Read: John 5:1-15

Record: Write down one verse from this passage that stood out to you.

Respond: Write a short prayer, talking to God about that verse.

*O*ne thing I love about the healing stories in the Bible ... Jesus deals with each person uniquely. Jesus talks theology with the Samaritan woman and acknowledges her sin without beating her over the head with lectures. He heals the official's son without any actual contact with the boy at all. In other passages, He tells us that God allowed the malady because the eventual joy and healing would bring glory to His Name and life to many who believed because of it. This case of our lame man is also unique. Jesus asks him what seems to be a rather odd question: "Would you like to get well?"

I've pondered that. It could mean a lot of different things. Was the man possibly enjoying his martyred status as the one who never reached the water first? Were people perhaps more likely to give him money and/or food simply because he'd been there the longest? Did the man have some  sin in his life that caused the initial sickness and subsequent lameness? I have no clue. But this I know: Jesus knew that man fully. He asked that question for a reason.

I wonder. When Jesus told the man to stand up, did the man ponder staying there in the familiarity of the place? Was that why Jesus had prepared the man by asking if he really wanted to be well again? You know, we can get "stuck" in a place of self-imposed martyrdom. We can maybe enjoy feeling pitied because we have had to put up with some trial or some difficult person. We can wear our tragedy like a badge of honor and kind of enjoy it in a weird way. Do we want to be well? Wellness means no more favored treatment and sympathetic looks. It means we need to work and serve and care for others instead of being the one who needs the care. Hmm ... being healthy comes with a cost.

Jesus had more words for our guy after he stood up and picked up his mat and walked. So did the Jewish leaders. They were upset he was carrying a mat on a Sabbath—a taboo in their long list of rules about Sabbath-keeping. As usual, they looked at the outside of the man and found the infraction of their rules. Jesus was concerned with his heart. "Now you are well; so stop sinning, or something even worse may happen to you" (v. 14). Well then. Something must have been "off" inside this man. It could have been his thought life. It could have been a deceiving spirit that exaggerated his pains to garner sympathy. It could have been a lazy streak, and he just plain didn't want to work. I don't need to know the answer. It's not my story. But I surely hope this healed man listened and ended up following the Lord Jesus because then he would be fully well. Inside and out.

God sees our hearts. God loves us even in our messy sinfulness. However, His heart for us is that we be the best we can be, fully surrendered to Him and fulfilling His good purposes for our lives. He wants us to live in fullness of joy, and that only happens when we allow Him to point out our sins and flaws and ask Him to change us. Let's look to Him for full healing!

My verse: "But afterward Jesus found him in the temple and told him, 'Now you are well; so stop sinning, or something even worse may happen to you'" (John 5:14).

My response: Lord, You know our thoughts and hearts. You see our motives and every evil inclination of our hearts. What was it about this man, that he needed this warning and rebuke? Thank You that You know uniquely what each of us needs.

John 5:16-30

Request: Thank You, Lord, for today. You've given me life and this small space of time to just sit at Your feet and learn. Help me to treasure this and not waste it. In Jesus' Name, Amen.

Read: John 5:16-30

Record: Write down one verse from this passage that stood out to you.

Respond: Write a short prayer, talking to God about that verse.

_____

_____

_____

_____

_____

_____

_____

_____

*J*esus was getting an earful from the Jewish leaders in this section, wasn't He? They were fixated on a healed man carrying a mat. So strange, isn't it? A man who had not walked in 38 years . . . *walked*. You'd think that would get them at least a little bit curious about Jesus, the Healer. But no. Their "god" was their rulebook, and the rulebook said No Carrying Things on Sabbath. Do we ever get fixated on the wrong things? Are we ever so passionate about an issue that we cease to see good in a person who might disagree with us? God is adamant in the Ten Commandments that there shall be no other gods before Him and this, I believe, is why: When we start valuing anything or anyone higher than God, our whole view of life becomes terribly distorted. He is the only One who deserves first place, and when He is lifted high, all of life is ordered as it should be.

I love how Jesus answered the Jewish leaders. It's so simple: "[The Son] does only what he sees the Father doing" (v. 19). His directions come directly from God, who, after all, invented the Ten Commandments and fully understands every nuanced application. Jesus models for us  the life we too can live—a listening life. His heart was to fulfill the purpose for which He came and that meant doing the Father's will every single moment. None of us are that selfless. None of us love God so much that all of our thoughts and desires are centered on pleasing Him. But the closer we grow to that state, ironically, the more "us" we are. God doesn't ask us to turn into little obedient clones of each other. He isn't making us into identical robots all looking exactly alike. After all, He made the hummingbird *and* the giraffe. He's creative to the point even snowflakes are unique. Yes, we are to "look like Him" but that doesn't rob us of the unique DNA He gave us. We are fearfully and wonderfully knit together. Hallelujah! He wired us to "work best" when we are connected to Him in our own little unique place in the world.

Jesus also pulled no punches about who He was. Anyone with ears to hear heard that He was God in flesh, come to save the world. Let's look at His statements together:

> *"For just as the Father gives life to those he raises from the dead, so the Son gives life to anyone he wants."* —John 5: 21

> *"... he [God] has given the Son absolute authority to judge."* —John 5:22b

> *"... Anyone who does not honor the Son is certainly not honoring the Father who sent him."* —John 5:23b

> *"I tell you the truth, those who listen to my message and believe in God who sent me have eternal life ...."* —John 5:24a

> *"The Father has life in himself, and he has granted that same life-giving power to his Son."* —John 5:26

> *"And he has given him authority to judge everyone because he is the Son of Man."* —John 5:27

There's more, of course, but wow! Jesus is the judge and the life-giver. He declares it clearly. So, His answer to the breaking-of-the-Sabbath question is basically that He did what the One who gave the Sabbath rule told Him to do. And that supersedes any silly interpretation of the law these leaders chose to give it.  The Author of the Law gets to make the rules for the law, right? John is helping us see who Jesus is. And Jesus is the majestic, Holy One, Messiah, Son of Man predicted in Daniel 7. Those who were truly looking for truth back then found Him, and those who are truly looking for truth today also find Him because He wants to gather us to Himself.

My verse: "'I tell you the truth, those who listen to my message and believe in God who sent me have eternal life. They will never be condemned for their sins, but they have already passed from death to life'" (John 5:24).

My response: Lord, help me to live life as one who has already passed from death to life. At some point, You will come for me and take my spirit out of an old, broken-down body and give me a new one. My earthly shell of a body will crumble, but I myself will not die. I will simply step into eternity. Death has truly lost its sting. Hallelujah!

John 5:31-47

Request: Lord, I am so thankful for this opportunity to hear from You. Speak to me, please, as I seek how best to live my days for You in ways that matter eternally. In Jesus' Name, Amen.

Read: John 5:31-47

Record: Write down one verse from this passage that stood out to you.

Respond: Write a short prayer, talking to God about that verse.

_____

_____

_____

_____

_____

_____

_____

_____

*W*e now finish up Jesus' response to the Jewish leaders. John records all of it for us so we can see just how clearly Jesus told these leaders who He was. I am especially drawn to verse 34. "'Of course, I have no need of human witnesses, but I say these things so you might be saved.'" Isn't that just so kind? These leaders, who are being super picky and critical, are so loved by Jesus that He still wants them saved. He patiently shares with them who He is, reminds them that John the Baptist pointed to Him, and refers them to the testimony of His miracles and His own words . . . because He wants them to be saved.

His desire is for all of us to come to Him. He's interested in one obscure Samaritan woman, far removed from what most would consider a moral life, and He's interested in these puffed-up Jewish leaders who, despite their outward morality, are not truly looking for God at all. How patient He is as He explains. How firm He is at some points, trying to wake them up to see the truth. They are nitpicking at God-in-flesh, Messiah! They are judging the One who made them and who will someday truly judge them. Oh, how He wants them to see the truth!

Have you ever been in a position where you desperately wanted a loved one to see the truth about Jesus? I have. It's so hard to talk to someone whose mind has closed to the possibility that God could be real. It seems impossible for us to wake them up, but it is not impossible for God. I pray often that God would open eyes and unstop ears so that my loved ones, who do not yet recognize Him, will have that beautiful "aha!" moment when they truly realize that God is there and cares deeply about them. Never stop praying, friend. Never stop asking God to move in a stubborn heart.

I've seen God change a heart that was closed to Him for over 90 years. Yes, 90 years! Also, I had a Sunday school teacher once, whose wife prayed for him for 40 years before he finally saw the truth that he was made on purpose by the God who loves him! As he made up for lost time and shared his faith with us sixth-grade Sunday schoolers, His teaching was vibrant and passionate. I believe that every time we pray, God moves. He won't kick down a door. He allows us the dignity of choosing whether or not to open it to Him. But, as we ask Him, He will continue to reveal Himself in the lives of those who need Him and just don't realize it yet.

My verse: "'You search the Scriptures because you think they give you eternal life. But the Scriptures point to me!'" (John 5:39).

My response: Lord, help me to keep this distinction. Yes, the Bible is Your Word. But it isn't You. These words draw me to You, a living Being who was and is and always will be. Parsing verses and examining nuance without prayer and a heart to know You? It's not going to be life-giving. Only You give eternal life. The Bible leads me to You, but I am not to worship the Bible. I worship You alone.

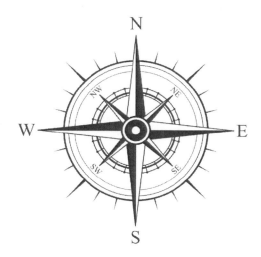

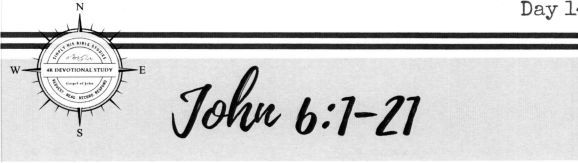

John 6:1-21

Request: Dear Lord, please teach me today as I come to listen and learn. In Jesus' Name, Amen.

Read: John 6:1-21

Record: Write down one verse from this passage that stood out to you.

Respond: Write a short prayer, talking to God about that verse.

*D*id you notice the reference to Passover in this chapter? In verse 4, John lets us know it's almost time for Passover again. He mentioned the first Passover Jesus celebrated during His public ministry years in chapter two. Now, we have the sec- ond Passover. John's record shows us that time is passing and enables us to know with a fair degree of certainty that Jesus' time on Earth as a man was about three years. The final Passover ends with His crucifixion and resurrection.

As Jesus continues to heal the hurt and the sick and the broken, not everyone is as stubborn as our Jewish leaders after seeing His miracles. He is attracting large crowds. This is a bit of a problem, isn't it? Alone time with the disciples would have been much harder to come by and imagine having people—masses of people—following you and watching you all the time. That sounds a bit uncomfortable to me. Our story today featured a crowd of thousands. The men alone accounted for 5,000, but probably as many women and children were there as well. Jesus not only taught them, He fed them. All of them. With just five loaves and two fish. What a phe- nomenal miracle!

It's no wonder that people wanted to make Jesus a king on the spot. Free food? Healing from sicknesses? What's not to love? But I love how Jesus just calmly slipped away. The peace that He carried with Him was amazing. The crowds didn't disturb it at all—even when they were trying to force Him into kingship! The fierce gale on the lake didn't disturb His peace. He just walked on out to the boat on the water, and then "there they were" at their destination. Jesus knew that every minute of His life was planned by God and that He was quite safe as He followed God's directions. He had no need for fear or anxiety ever.

The same is true for you and me if we belong to Him. Even in the gales of life, He is always with us, and we can find our rest in that. I long for peace like that. My heart's desire is to follow God so closely that nothing rattles me. I know times of sorrow and pain will come, but I'd love to be done with times of panic and anxiety! One simple practice has helped so much with my tendency to worry and fret. As soon as fear or worry enters my mind, I turn it into a prayer. For example, if my husband does not come home on time, and I can't reach him by phone, I imagine all sorts of terrible things. Was he in a car accident? Did he fall and break a leg with no one around to help? If I allow these thoughts to continue, I can easily become panicked. So, the antidote is to immediately stop and pray. Right then. I ask God for His help and protection for my husband wherever he is. Praying is the best thing I can do. I can then rest, knowing that I've asked the all-powerful God to help me and my hubby. The act of praying reminds me that God is with my husband and even if the worst happens, I can trust that He allowed it. In this example, sure enough, home comes my husband with a reminder that he had told me he would be in a meeting and back late—and I had forgotten. [Sigh] Worry is such a waste of emotional energy, isn't it? And it certainly never solved anyone's problems. If we linger in a state of worry, our anxiety just grows bigger. Let's listen to our Father like Jesus did and trust God with the gales, the crowds, and all the problems that are bound to enter our lives. *Lord, give us Your peace in the midst of our storms, please!*

My verse: "But he called out to them, 'Don't be afraid. I am here!'" (John 6:20).

My response: Lord, this is such a beautiful example of Your love. Like a parent when a child is afraid or my dear husband, Ray, hugging me after a nightmare, You soothe us simply by Your Presence. And You are always . . . present! Help me to remember: Don't be afraid. You're right here with me.

John 6:22-40

Request: Thank You for these quiet moments, Lord, when I can sit with You and remember that You are with me always. You know me so well, Father, so I ask You to show me what I need today as I read Your Word. In Jesus' Name, Amen.

Read: John 6:22-40

Record: Write down one verse from this passage that stood out to you.

Respond: Write a short prayer, talking to God about that verse.

_____

_____

_____

_____

_____

_____

_____

*O*h, my goodness. That crowd is persistent. They notice that the disciples have taken off without Jesus, so people start looking for Him. They are so confused when they find Him on the far shore and can't figure out how He got there. He does not enlighten them. He knows people's hearts, and He sees that they are not understanding the purpose of these miracles. The purpose is to show them that God the Son has come to Earth. They're just interested in the free food and the spectacular miracles that are super fun to watch. Jesus is not someone they want to follow and obey. He's more like an entertainer to them. They want Him to do things their way. They have no intention of bowing to Him and declaring Him their Lord and Savior.

So, Jesus who loved the Samaritan woman and who loved the Jewish leaders, now speaks out of love for this errant, sensation-seeking crowd. He tells them bluntly, "*I am the bread of life*" (v. 35). And He urges them to come to Him—not to see His miracles, but to know Him, the God who saves and who loves them. He tells them that He has something to offer far more valuable than mere bread that only fills the stomach temporarily. He offers them eternal life. Oh, how He wants them to see how much more He has to give them than just eating and looking for the latest thrill.

Times haven't changed all that much, have they? Too many of us even today live for a good meal and the latest thrill. We give scant thought to what happens after we die, even though that has to be one of the most important questions on the planet. It's okay to enjoy life here. It's a good thing to be grateful for good food and fun experiences. But we can't live just for the next temporary thrill.

We are going to spend eternity somewhere. We were made for larger purposes than we can fathom, not just in this life but in the life to come. We too need to come to Jesus, the Bread of Life, and ask Him for sustenance that lasts.

My verses: "Jesus told them, 'This is the only work God wants from you: Believe in the one he has sent'" (John 6:29). "'For it is my Father's will that all who see his Son and believe in him should have eternal life. I will raise them up at the last day'" (John 6:40).

My response: These two verses tell such an amazing story, Lord! My "work" is simply to believe. All other work has been completed by Your Son on my behalf. It's Your will that I should have eternal life—Eden restored—paradise with You. Wow. It makes me want to work for You, even though I am not saved by my works. Help me to please You in all I do.

Jesus spoke to the people once more and said, "I am the light of the world. If you follow me, you won't have to walk in darkness, because you will have the light that leads to life."

— JOHN 8:12 —

WEEK FOUR

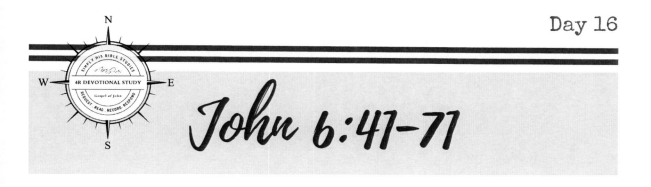

John 6:41-71

Request: Dear Lord Jesus, I thank You for being the Bread of Life. Today, I want to feast on what matters: Your words in the Bible. Nourish me. Fill me with what is good and noble and true so I am satisfied and able to go out and serve You fully. In Your Name, Amen.

Read: John 6:41-71

Record: Write down one verse from this passage that stood out to you.

Respond: Write a short prayer, talking to God about that verse.

*T*his is a hard passage to understand. At least, I think it is. So did many of Jesus' followers. His words about eating His flesh and drinking His blood sounded so . . . odd and perhaps revolting . . . that they walked away. Trying to understand God and His plans for us will always be a bit of a mystery.

Think of it this way: Let's say we have a colony of ants busily creating new tunnels and safe places for ant babies to be born. Unbeknownst to them, just where our little ants are busy, plans are being made to flood the area and create a reservoir. Let's say a human comes along who loves ants and wants to help them escape to higher ground. The only way to communicate is to become an ant and speak "ant" talk. Which, let's be real, is probably quite limited. Would a human in ant form be able to adequately explain this complex thought to these tiny creatures happy in their current colony? It would be a stretch.

Well. God is bigger by far than that human ant-lover, and compared to God, we are way smaller than ants. Jesus speaks truth. He speaks of matters that are still a bit of a mystery to us. He explains heavenly concepts to earth-bound creatures. He unpacks mysteries. One of those mysteries is this idea of needing Jesus so much that we want to ingest His flesh and drink His blood.

We do this symbolically in Communion. When we receive Him as Lord and Savior, He does enter us in some mysterious way, and His Spirit lives within us. Beyond that? I can't explain this passage to you. It's comforting to me, though, to realize He desires for us to want Him *that much*. It's comforting to me that I do not understand everything because that underlines for me who is God (Jesus, God in flesh) and who is not (that would be me, Sharon!). I stand with Peter in this. Jesus is the way, the truth, and the life. To turn from Him is to turn from light to darkness, hope to despair. Where else can we go except to the Savior? I will trust Him when I don't understand and patiently wait for Him to reveal to me all I need to know as I grow in Him. How about you?

My verse: "'For no one can come to me unless the Father who sent me draws them to me, and at the last day I will raise them up'" (John 6:44).

My response: Lord, thank You for the reminder that my witnessing to others is not successful based on "works"—how smart or persuasive I am. Jesus shared hard-to-understand truths and the people complained. He still rested in the fact that You alone are the One who converts and draws people to Yourself. I can rest in that as well.

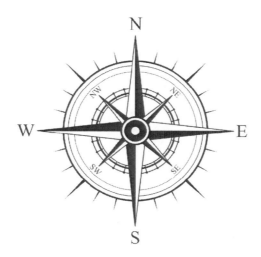

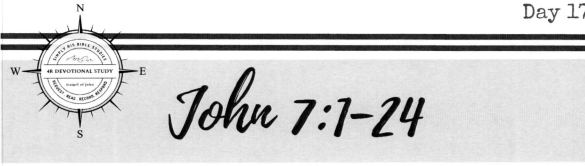

John 7:1-24

Request: Dear Father, here I am. Teach me, please. Open my eyes to see what You would show me from Your Word. In Jesus' Name, Amen.

Read: John 7:1-24

Record: Write down one verse from this passage that stood out to you.

Respond: Write a short prayer, talking to God about that verse.

*W*e leave the long talk about bread and move on to Jesus' travels around Galilee. How sad to see that—at this point in time—Jesus' brothers do not believe He is Messiah. They even goad Him to "prove" Himself, like Satan did when Jesus was in the wilderness. Jesus pays no attention. He has an agenda given to Him by God, and that's the only one that matters. Oh, I need to be more like Jesus! I am too easily influenced by people who think I should do this or that thing and pressure me to do so.

Have you ever been pressured to do something—even a good something—but not necessarily what you ought to be doing? I surely have. When I see a need at church, and I have the ability to meet that need, I can think having the ability means it's my responsibility. This is not true. I have plenty of abilities, and if I did all I could potentially do, I would never sleep or see my husband! There are always more good things to do than time to do them. Like Jesus, we need to meet with God regularly and ask *Him* to reveal which duties are "ours," right? That means He may sometimes ask us to do more than we wish. I have a new friend right now because God told me to get to know her, even though I felt "too busy" for anyone new in my life. I could barely keep up with my current friends. Yet, this friend has been a rich blessing and gift to me. I am so glad I heard His voice urging me to make time for her.

Other times, though, He's pulled me back from legitimately good opportunities. I could have done them, but I've said "no" because God knew I needed more space in my life for other good things. This is living by the Spirit. It's taking every opportunity to the Lord in prayer and asking Him to help with the decision-making. Sometimes, He's really clear and sometimes it's harder, and I ask godly friends to pray with me and help me. But, just like Jesus, we need to have one agenda: What does God want us to do?

I love that Jesus ended up going to the festival later in the week, evidently when God told Him to go! I love His answers to the accusing folk who didn't believe in Him. He never tried to draw attention to Himself as much as He pointed to His Father. He wanted people to see God in Him and through Him, but His desire on Earth was to model for us the way to live—yielding to God at every turn.

I think His answer to the accusers about healing on the Sabbath was very clever. Oh, rules can be sticky things. Yes, it is good to take one day in seven and rest. God commands it. God showed it by example when He rested on the seventh day. It's good for body and soul to rest. But when we take that rule to extremes, we can potentially cause great damage to others. What would happen to those who were hit by earthquakes or tornadoes if we all ignored them on Sabbath and went about our own sweet resting? No, when a pressing need arises, we meet it. And then we go back to resting. That's Spirit-led living as opposed to rules-based living.

And the only way to live by the Spirit is to stay close to God. You, dear reader, are working toward that with every day you take time to meet with Him and learn more through His Word. When you make that little "time sacrifice" and stop the busy and sit at His feet, you are in a listening place where God can whisper His will to you! You might go days without hearing something specific, but you still meet with Him. You are available and ready for any word He has for you. If you don't stop to listen, how will you ever hear? I'm so glad you are doing this study with me!

My verses: "'For if the correct time for circumcising your son falls on the Sabbath, you go ahead and do it so as not to break the law of Moses. So why should you be angry with me for healing a man on the Sabbath? Look beneath the surface so you can judge correctly'" (John 7:23-24).

My response: Father, I need help in this area. I want to keep the rules all the time—perhaps at times when the kinder thing would be to help someone. You saw a man in pain, Lord Jesus, and "broke" the Sabbath law to do the great work of restoration. Help me to "look beneath the surface" to the heart of Your commandments, please. I want to hear Your voice and do Your will.

John 7:25-53

Request: Dear Holy God, I come to You today asking You to speak to me and teach me. Help me make the best choices in how to spend my days. Give me insight as I discern priorities. And Lord? Right now . . . I choose You as my priority. In Jesus' Name, Amen.

Read: John 7:25-53

Record: Write down one verse from this passage that stood out to you.

Respond: Write a short prayer, talking to God about that verse.

_____

_____

_____

_____

_____

_____

_____

*T*hings are heating up. Jesus is gaining traction among the people. Many are convinced that He is indeed the Messiah. This does not make the religious leaders happy. They are convinced that He is just a rabble-rouser and a liar. It's fascinating to read this passage and see the diversity of opinions about our Lord and Savior. Even today, people have diverse opinions about Him, don't they?

I laughed out loud when the guards came back without Jesus because they "never heard anyone speak like this!" (v. 46). Don't you wish you could have heard Jesus speak? Mark says repeatedly in his gospel that Jesus taught as one who had authority, not like the religious leaders. In that day, the favored way to talk about the law was to ask questions and then argue about it. That's what people were used to hearing. Various schools of thought existed among the rabbis, and those groups did not agree with each other, holding tightly to their own differing viewpoints. Then here comes Jesus, speaking confidently that He knows the answers. (Because He does!) No wonder the guards just walked away. I love it!

Let's talk about water. Jesus proclaims in this section of Scripture that "'Anyone who believes in me may come and drink! For the Scriptures declare, "Rivers of living water will flow from his heart"'" (v. 38). This isn't the first time He's offered "living water." Remember He shared this idea with the Samaritan woman at the well in John 4? Now He proclaims this idea to a much wider audience. We should pay special attention when Jesus repeats Himself.

Water is a vital substance. On every continent, in every culture, in every century, people need water. It's basic to life. Without water, we die in less than a week. Our bodies are comprised of about 60% water. That's a lot of water, right?

So now, let's look at Jesus' claim that He is "Living Water." That means He is essential. To every person born on every continent in every culture in every century. He is necessary for the sinful Samaritan women with all those husbands. He is necessary for the sinful religious leaders, who worried more about their own positions in the community than about truly exploring what Jesus said and who He was. He is necessary for all of us sinful people. Eternally, not one of us can live without Him. I love that He uses an illustration that relates to all of us, all around the globe. Missionaries can use it as they speak to even the most remote tribes. In every situation, it's understandable. Water and Jesus. Essential for Life. That should be on a T-shirt!

Oh, one more thought . . . I love that our shy Nicodemus spoke up and defended Jesus a wee bit. He's growing bolder!

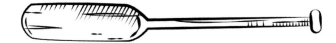

My verse: "While Jesus was teaching in the temple he called out, 'Yes, you know me, and you know where I come from. But I'm not here on my own. The one who sent me is true, and you don't know him'" (John 7:28).

My response: Jesus always points to the Father. He models what I want to do better—be constantly aware that I am God's girl, all of me. I'm not my own. I'm to act like I'm His, and to listen to His voice. Father, teach me to abide in You—always aware that You are with me and have a plan for me. Like Jesus—I'm not on my own. Thanks be to God!

John 8:1-20

Request: Thank You, Lord. Thank You for time to stop and be still. Thank You for Your love for me. Thank You for a quiet space where I can meet with You. Make me ready, please. In Jesus' Name, Amen.

Read: John 8:1-20

Record: Write down one verse from this passage that stood out to you.

Respond: Write a short prayer, talking to God about that verse.

*O*ur reading today has two very distinct and separate parts. Let's start with the woman caught in adultery. [Oy] That's a hard scene to picture. Who caught her? Where was the man she was committing adultery with? Had someone told the Pharisees about this or were they setting a trap? Perhaps so they could discredit Jesus? I don't know. I do know that it would have been all kinds of awful for her to be brought to the temple area in front of a large crowd and exhibited like that.

The Pharisees and religious leaders thought they'd found a way to hurt Jesus. The law of Moses said that men and women caught in adultery could be punished by stoning. Pretty severe. (Sidenote: God does not like adultery. A good thing to remember in any case.) However, under Roman law, only Rome could put a person to death. So, their question to Jesus does appear to be a trap. The religious leaders had no legal author-ity to put anyone to death, and they could cause a lot of trouble for themselves by stoning without Rome's stamp of approval. They knew the rules and so did the crowd. But there they were, chal-lenging Jesus to obey the Mosaic law. Or not. And either way, they thought Jesus would look bad.

But He didn't, did He? I love that He didn't even answer right away. He started writing in the dust. For centuries, scholars have wondered what He wrote. Many think He wrote words like Liar, Cheater, Envious, Sabbath-breaker, Idolater, Thief . . . possibly even specific sins of the accusers. All we know for sure is that His answer to them was to go ahead and stone her—but only if the one doing the stoning had never sinned. And that was that. Of course, they had all sinned. And whether it was their sins Jesus had written in the dirt or not, you can be sure God reminded their hearts of just how imperfect they truly were. And away they walked, leaving this vulnerable woman standing before Jesus.

I love that she called Him "Lord." I love that He didn't bother to lecture her. She knew what she'd done was wrong. She'd been deeply humiliated. He spoke eight words. "Neither do I. Go and sin no more" (v. 11). John did not forget Jesus' words. I suspect she never forgot them either, nor did those who watched.

You know, when we talk too much, pretty soon all we say turns into a giant blur of mush in the minds of our listeners. Especially if the talk is unpleasant. If we want to be heard . . . we should say less and say it well. This was a lesson I learned too late as a mother. Don't be like me. If you still have children at home, say less. And make sure what you say is wise and true. Even if your kids are grown, remember Jesus' brief, quiet words here. It will help in many an argument. When we say less . . . more is heard.

Jesus also gives another "I am" statement in our passage. He has already declared Himself to be the "Bread of Life." Now He announces that He is the "*Light of the World*" (v. 12)—a pretty bold claim. These words led C. S. Lewis to teach that Jesus was either a lunatic, a liar, or Lord of all. Good, nice teachers don't talk like that, do they? How long would you attend a church where the pastor declared He was the light of the world and you had to follow him in order to see?

Um. No. The people of Jesus' day had the same dilemma. Was He the One He said He was—the light of the entire world? The One who had seen God? The One who lived before Abraham? The One who told common folk to leave their jobs and follow Him? These are stunning, revolutionary words in any century.

Jesus doesn't allow us to think of Him in insipid, banal terms. He's bold. John wants us to hear Him in all His boldness and confidence. God put on flesh and walked among us, says John. And Jesus is truly the One He said He was. If we want to see, we need to go to Him, Light of the World, Creator of the sun, moon, and stars. He's that huge and that grand and that divine.

My verse: "They kept demanding an answer, so he stood up again and said, 'All right, but let the one who has never sinned throw the first stone!'" (John 8:7).

My response: Jesus, You didn't say the law was wrong, but Your mercy was right there, triumphing over judgment. You knew that every accuser was also a sinner. And then? Your beautiful answer to her, full of respect for the law (adultery is a grievous wrong, after all), combined with gentleness and grace: "Neither do I [condemn you]. Go and sin no more" (v. 11). Oh, what a tender, merciful response. No long lecture. Sin acknowledged. Mercy extended. Thank You, Lord, for Your beautiful kindness and forgiveness on display in this story!

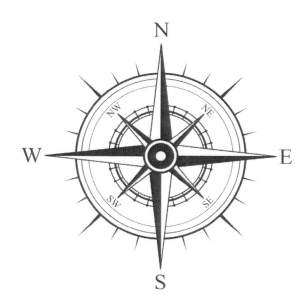

N
W E
S

John 8:21-32

Request: Dear Lord Jesus, I thank You for being the Light of the World. Oh, Lord, it's such a dark place . . . this world. We need Your light. Illumine my heart as I read Your Word and gather strength for the day, please. In Your Name, Amen.

Read: John 8:21-32

Record: Write down one verse from this passage that stood out to you.

Respond: Write a short prayer, talking to God about that verse.

*a*s I read this passage in preparation for this study, I needed to stop and put myself into the scene. Here is a group of people created by Jesus. He is standing in front of them, and they are not quite "getting it" as He talks to them. And He wants them to "get it" and choose Him. He speaks persuasively and with great firmness. ". . . You will die in your sins; for unless you believe that I AM who I claim to be, you will die in your sins" (v. 24). Can you imagine the grief He must have felt looking at them? "Wake up! Before it's too late! Turn to Me so I can help you." That is what He's saying.

Have you ever watched someone make choices you knew were going to hurt them, and they just wouldn't listen? Perhaps they were going to a party, and you knew their purpose was to get drunk. Perhaps they were taking drugs or deciding to joy ride without headlights or seatbelts fastened. "Don't do this," you beg. And yet they do. Jesus wasn't predicting that something bad *might* happen. He *knew* that they would die in their sins unless they turned and believed.

He then says something remarkable. He predicts His death on the cross. This is stated explicitly in the *Amplified Bible* and in the *New Living Translation*. Other translations say only that He will be "lifted up." As He looks at these lost sheep, mired and bent down by past and present sins, unable to live without condemnation and shame, He looks ahead to the coming rescue. He will make a way of escape if only those lis-tening to Him remember His words and turn to Him in the days ahead. Because He loves them, He warns them. He was always pointing them to God the Father. He wants them set free. Even at that time, John writes that many believed in Jesus.

I love Jesus' statement that the truth will set you free. It will! Lies and deceptions never bring freedom. They bring bondage. As soon as we tell a lie, we have to remember we told it, and then protect it by other things we say. Our mind is cluttered with the subterfuge and the fear of being found out. If we "live a lie" and pretend we are perfect and all is always well, we also are not living truthfully. We all struggle, and it really is smarter to just admit it. Then, we can point to our great need for our great God to rescue us!

When we tell the truth and live in truth, we have nothing to hide. And the greatest truth is that God so loved the world He gave His Son to die and take the punishment we deserve on Himself so that we might live . . . free. We are not under condemnation. We are not under guilt and shame once we've come to Him. He's paid the price in full for our foolish, sinful ways and washed us clean and fresh and new again. Oh, praise God! That is freedom indeed.

My verse: "'That is why I said that you will die in your sins; for unless you believe that I AM who I claim to be, you will die in your sins'" (John 8:24).

My response: Oh, how You warned those back then and how You warn us now! We have a way out. We don't have to die in our sins. You came to rescue us. Our part is simply to believe and receive the rescue. Thank You. Oh! How You love us!

"I am the good shepherd. The good shepherd sacrifices his life for the sheep."

— JOHN 10:11 —

W E E K   F I V E

John 8:33-59

Request: Dear Father, here I am, Your little one. Would You please teach and lead me today as I read? Thank You. In Jesus' Name, I ask this, Amen.

Read: John 8:33-59

Record: Write down one verse from this passage that stood out to you.

Respond: Write a short prayer, talking to God about that verse.

*I*n his book, *Mere Christianity*, C. S. Lewis writes about the impossibility of Jesus being a "great moral teacher." Many people, trying to be nice and polite, but not really wanting to engage Christianity, feel that it's appropriate to relegate Jesus to the ranks of nice, historical figures who said good things. "Oh, I don't know that He was God, but He was certainly a great moral teacher," they say. Lewis replies that a careful reading of Jesus' actual words, as reported by eyewitnesses like our John, absolutely rules that out. Even great moral teachers don't say what Jesus said. Today's passage is a fantastic example. Think about a pastor you know or a great moral person who loves God. Can you imagine them making any of these statements?

"I am telling you what I saw when I was with my Father . . . ." —John 8:38a

". . . I have come to you from God. I am not here on my own, but he sent me." —John 8:42b

"I tell you the truth, anyone who obeys my teaching will never die!" —John 8:51

"Your father Abraham rejoiced as he looked forward to my coming. He saw it and was glad." —John 8:56

". . . I tell you the truth, before Abraham was even born, I AM!" —John 8:58b

The last passage I quoted was so obviously a claim that Jesus was God Himself that the people listening picked up stones to throw at Him. They knew right away He was calling Himself by the sacred and holy Name of God—Yahweh—I AM—a name they would not even say out loud.

So, back to our great moral teacher. How long would you stay around if a pastor started telling you he was Yahweh? Or that all you had to do was obey him and you would live forever? Yeah. You wouldn't. He'd either be a liar or a lunatic. Or . . . he'd be telling the truth and would be Lord of all. And that, posits C. S. Lewis, is exactly who Jesus is. Lord of all. He proclaimed it because it is true. He was not simply a great moral teacher.

John wants us to hear, loud and clear, all the declarations of Jesus that set Him apart from all other rabbis and teachers of His time (and of all time!). John wants us to know that the One who loves us is not just a nice, moral man, but God come to us in human form as the Son of Man and Son of God. It's that big and that grand and that supernatural. It's that wonderful.

One other section in this passage I'd like to mention is when Jesus describes the devil as a murderer and a liar. Jesus says the devil is the "father of lies." If you remember back to his lie in the Garden of Eden, you see how apt that name is. He told Adam and Eve, "you won't die!" (Genesis 3:4a). Adam and Eve surely did die. Satan lied then, and he will always lie. He hates the truth and the light. Bargaining with the devil or even listening to him is always a bad idea. Nothing good will come from it. I once knew a woman who refused to step into a ministry position because she feared the devil would then attack her. Very tragically, she was attacked anyway and faced many hardships. You can't bargain with the devil. He's a liar from the beginning. How much better it would have been for my friend if she had said a "yes" to God, and then, when the attacks came, she would have had the close companionship of ministry people who loved Jesus surrounding her in a special way. God helped her in any case because our God is so good like that! He's always there for the lost and hurting. But I never forgot that her "no" did not save her from trouble. Several times in my own life I have been faced with hard situations, and I was so very glad to be in a ministry with people who truly prayed for me. That was God's sweet provision prepared in advance for me. I'm so grateful.

My verse: "Jesus answered, 'I tell you the truth, before Abraham was even born, I AM!'" (John 8:58).

My response: Lord Jesus, You told them flat out who You were—who You are and always will be—very God in flesh—always existent. In this lengthy exchange, they were told, and Your words were so clear. But they didn't believe You. You were no ordinary man. You existed before Abraham. You are the Word. The Holy One. And I worship You.

LOVED. A BIBLE STUDY

John 9:1-23

Request: Dear Lord Jesus, I worship You this morning as truly Son of God, and I am in awe of what You did for us when You lived among us for a while. Teach me, please, as I read Your Word this morning. In Your Name, Amen.

Read: John 9:1-23

Record: Write down one verse from this passage that stood out to you.

Respond: Write a short prayer, talking to God about that verse.

_____

_____

_____

_____

_____

_____

_____

*W*e come now to another miracle. John tells far fewer miracle stories than Matthew, Mark, or Luke. But when he does tell a story, he lingers over it and gives us details and nuance. We have the opportunity to see this particular miracle—healing a man blind since birth—up close and in great detail.

First, it's important to realize that this man had never been able to see. It wasn't like he had an eye injury that just took a while to heal and "happened" to heal just when Jesus appeared. Nope. He was blind from birth, and Jesus gave him sight. Wow.

 Second, Jesus stops the notion that if a child is born with a birth defect it is because his parents did something wrong. Have you ever heard someone bemoan a hardship and cry out, "What did I do to deserve this"? Why do we think we are in control of all the good or bad things that happen to us? Bad things happen because we live on a fallen planet where sin is abundant and life has gone off-kilter. But being born with a handicap is not because our parents sinned. God allows it for a reason. And in this man's case, it was to have the honor of being a sign to the world that Messiah had come!

I find it interesting that Jesus chose to have the blind man participate in his healing. Jesus could have just touched his eyes. Jesus could have just spoken, and sight would have returned. We've seen Him do that in other miracles. But Jesus' miracles fit each person, not a predictable pattern. He deals with people as the unique individuals they are. And this blind man, who ended up declaring some pretty powerful truths about Jesus, had a role to play in his healing—he had to go wash the mud off his eyes. I wonder if part of the reason was so he could gradually adjust to the shock of sight. He knew in advance to expect it, and as he washed, sight appeared. Perhaps it was a kindness to him as he took in the barrage of color and shapes never before seen or imagined!

Third and last, let's look at the response of the people, the religious leaders, and the blind man's parents. Those who witnessed this miracle had a hard time believing it. That makes sense to me.

People who are blind from birth don't suddenly see. And yet here was this blind man now able to see. It takes time for us to grasp when something supernatural has taken place. Sadly, these witnesses took the man to the Pharisees, not with rejoicing but with a sort of tattletale approach. Jesus was walking along on the Sabbath when He encountered this man. And, of course, Jesus healed him. But this was deemed an "offense," which surely shows us how far the Sabbath laws had deteriorated from the days when they were first instituted. God tells us in Exodus 16, "They must realize that the Sabbath is the LORD's gift . . . "(Exodus 16:29a). It was meant to be a sweet present from God, this resting from labor and everyday work. It was never intended as a time to stop being kind when a person in need literally crossed your very path. Good grief!

The Pharisees' sad response was to badger this healed man and try to find a way to blame Jesus. No rejoicing that a man had been healed. Only questions asked and a decision made—Jesus could not be from God because He'd healed on the Sabbath. The parents' response was a fearful one and further shows us the power the Pharisees had over the people. They ducked the question and left their son to fend for himself. The text gives no indication they were happy he was healed. I have to believe they were, though, right?

My verse: "'We must quickly carry out the tasks assigned us by the one who sent us. The night is coming, and then no one can work'" (John 9:4).

My response: Lord, I have questions about this verse. Jesus says "we" and not "I." Is Jesus referring to Himself and the Holy Spirit? And, You, God, as the One who sent "us"? Is this a plural like the one in Genesis 1:26 where it reads, "Let us make man in our image"? And what does "the night is coming" mean, that from the time of Jesus' death until Pentecost no one will be healed? Did Jesus sense Your call to heal a man in need even though it was the Sabbath day of rest? Within these questions are my guesses, but, Lord, You are so much bigger and wiser than my mind can understand or comprehend.

N

W　**E**

S

SIMPLY HIS BIBLE STUDIES
4R DEVOTIONAL STUDY
Gospel of John
REQUEST · READ · RECORD · RESPOND

John 9:24-41

Request: Heavenly Father, how good it is to have this time of stillness with You this morning. Open my eyes that I might see what You have prepared for me today from Your Word. Feed me, please. In Jesus' Name, Amen.

Read: John 9:24-41

Record: Write down one verse from this passage that stood out to you.

Respond: Write a short prayer, talking to God about that verse.

*O*h, didn't you just love the blind man's wisdom as he parried with the Pharisees? I am so glad John chose to include this part of the story because it is an admirable lesson to us in courage. This newly-seeing man lost his rights to the synagogue because of his words, but he spoke truth as he saw it, didn't he? He did not just blindly (pun intended!) follow his leaders. He thought about it. He reflected on the character of God. And he concluded that Jesus must be from God. Let's look at his main argument together: "'We know that God doesn't listen to sinners, but he is ready to hear those who worship him and do his will. Ever since the world began, no one has been able to open the eyes of someone born blind. If this man were not from God, he couldn't have done it'" (vv. 31-33).

His declaration that Jesus must be from God was rewarded. Jesus came and found him. I love that Jesus followed up with him, don't you? Jesus cares about people. He doesn't just heal so that everyone will know He is God. He healed because He loved. And He clearly loved our blind man who  now could see. Jesus sought him out on purpose to tell him who He was. To this new believer— so that he could believe more fully—Jesus declared Himself to be the Son of Man. ("Son of Man" refers to Daniel 7:13, a unique reference found nowhere else in the Bible. Scholars then and now know that "Son of Man" is a name for Messiah.)

What did our now-seeing friend do when Jesus affirmed His authority as Messiah? John tells us that he did what we all should do: He worshiped Jesus. Here's another good reason to believe Jesus was not just a "good, moral teacher" as we talked about earlier. Jesus *allowed* the worship. That could only be right if He is God. Which, of course, He is.

Some Pharisees were still lurking about during this exchange. Jesus did not speak these words in secret, whispering them in a corner. He was also heard by the Pharisees. I find it interesting that Jesus did not condemn them for being "blind" to the truth. He condemned them for their pride, for claiming they could see. Over and over in the Bible, God consistently makes it clear that He is not pleased with prideful people. James 4:6a tells us that "God opposes the proud," and Proverbs 16:5a says, "The LORD detests the proud." Guess why? At least part of the reason is that when we are prideful and full of ourselves, no room is left in our lives for the God who loves us. We are best when we are humble and leaning on Him. When yoked with God, we can be all we are meant to be!

Let's humble ourselves before Him each day, remembering how much He has given us and how much we need Him. Let's be brave when it comes to speaking the truth about the Lord. Yesterday, I was asked by a neighbor I don't know well, "Are you religious?" It was with great joy that I could answer, "I am a Christian. I follow Jesus Christ." Let's declare Him as we are given opportunities. The days are short. People need to know Him.

My verse: "We know that God doesn't listen to sinners, but he is ready to hear those who worship him and do his will" (John 9:31).

My response: This whole dialogue fascinates me! I see why You set this man apart to be born blind ". . . so that the power of God could be seen in him" (v. 3). He's brilliant! He knows the Scriptures. He's articulate. And he is ready and eager to worship You, Lord. I also love that John tells his story so thoroughly.

John 10:1-21

Request: Father-God, what an honor it is to sit here and meet with You, King of kings, the One who controls the armies of Heaven and who holds the world in His hands. Please give me ears to hear You this morning. In Jesus' Name, Amen.

Read: John 10:1-21

Record: Write down one verse from this passage that stood out to you.

Respond: Write a short prayer, talking to God about that verse.

_____

_____

_____

_____

_____

_____

_____

*Y*ou know, I've always looked at the discourse on the Good Shepherd and His sheep as a separate entity, but it's most likely a continuation of the conversation with the blind man and the Pharisees. Chapters and verses were added later to the books of the Bible. When John wrote his gospel, there were no chapters. So, let's look at this section about sheep and shepherds in light of where we've just been—with Jesus telling the Pharisees that they are guilty because they claim to see when they are blind and . . . in need of a Shepherd.

We see here two more "I am" statements. Jesus declares Himself to be both the gate and the shepherd in this passage. First, He tells us, *"I am the gate"* (v. 7), the only way into safe pasture. We have to "come in" through Him if we want to be saved. This salvation is pictured beautifully in Jesus' words that when we enter by the Gate, we will "come and go freely and will find good pastures" (v. 9), but only when we enter by the Gate, who is Jesus. And His purpose is so wonderful: "My purpose is to give . . . a rich and satisfying life" (v. 10). Other translations call it an "abundant life." We are being invited to choose Him and His way to God. It's the only way. Trying to find God by scaling walls and sneaking in won't work. He is the Gate that opens to us eternal life—and abundant life.

Second, He reveals to us, *"I am the good shepherd"* (v. 11). He's not a hired man, like perhaps some of the religious leaders are, only in it for the paycheck. No. The sheep are His very own, and He cares for them. He calls them by name, and they know His voice. There's an intimacy between a shepherd and His sheep that is rich and beautiful. If you've ever watched a video—or maybe seen a shepherd calling his sheep, you'll know what I mean. They come running to the shepherd's voice. They know he feeds them, helps with their cuts and bruises, and has their very best interests at heart.

I love that Jesus looks ahead to the time when the flock will expand. "I have other sheep, too, that are not in this sheepfold. I must bring them also. They will listen to my voice, and there will be one flock with one shepherd" (v. 16). I think that He just might be referring to . . . us! Those of us who are Gentiles and believers, living long after the days Jesus walked the Earth. He waits to return for that last and final Second Coming until believers from every tribe and nation are gathered into the fold. How eager I am to one day see our Shepherd face to face!

My verse: "'I am the good shepherd; I know my own sheep, and they know me, just as my Father knows me and I know the Father . . .'" (John 10:14-15a).

My response: Father, You know me inside and out like no one else does. You know my thoughts, my heart, my history, my weaknesses, my very DNA. The fact that I am Yours and You want to know me is stunning. Please help me to know You more and more.

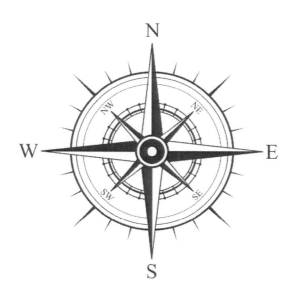

John 10:22-42

Request: So here I am, Lord and Shepherd of my soul, Your little lamb, eager to hear from You today. Speak to my heart and help me to hear and to follow Your voice. In Jesus' Name, Amen.

Read: John 10:22-42

Record: Write down one verse from this passage that stood out to you.

Respond: Write a short prayer, talking to God about that verse.

_____

_____

_____

_____

                           _____

                           _____

                           _____

                           _____

We have a location change now. John lets us know it's wintertime and that Jesus is in Jerusalem during Hanukkah. Isn't that the coolest? Jews all over the world still celebrate Hanukkah today, and Jesus did too. It's fun to think of Jesus enjoying the lighting of the candles each night and remembering with His disciples the miracle of the oil that did not run out for eight nights even though there was only enough left for one night. I love that John helps orient us to the time of year—and that he remembers the celebration times he had with Jesus.

Once again, the topic is sheep. Jesus again refers to Himself as a Shepherd, and He says one of the most reassuring statements in all of Scripture: "I give them eternal life, and they will never perish. No one can snatch them away from me, for my Father has given them to me, and he is more powerful than anyone else. No one can snatch them from the Father's hand" (vv. 28-29). I love that belonging to Jesus means I am safe. No one can take me away from Him. And that's that.

It's disturbing, though, to hear the people asking Jesus to speak plainly about whether or not He is the Messiah. He's told them over and over in various ways that He is. Still, they keep asking Him, and then either they don't believe it or they try to stone Him. Good grief. It's getting harder and harder for Jesus to speak and teach and heal in public with the rabble-rousers crowding around  and stirring up trouble. He patiently explains again that He and the Father are one, and that He has done miraculous works to show them His deity. However, they aren't interested in Him actually being Messiah. They either want to see Him perform miracles or they want to see Him arrested. [Sigh]

So, Jesus leaves. He goes back to the area where He began about three years before. He goes to the wilderness where John the Baptist lived and preached and baptized. John writes that Jesus "stayed there awhile" (v. 40). Perhaps He needed the relative quiet although many followed Him even there. Perhaps, He needed more solitude with God the Father as He prepared for His ultimate sacrifice coming that very year. I love that the Bible often mentions wilderness times. Moses spent 40 years in the wilderness as a shepherd himself before God called him to defy Pharoah and free his people. Abraham wandered in that same wilderness many years before that time. David spent time in the wilderness hiding from Saul, and Elijah also had a few years of wilderness living when a famine engulfed the land. Then right after His baptism, Jesus was led by the Spirit into the wilderness. Even Paul, when he received Christ, was led to Arabia for a season. God sometimes needs to separate us from normal life and tutor us intensely. It might not be Arabia, but we also experience times of loneliness or illness or suffering when we have limited resources and must learn to look to the Lord alone for our strength.

My verse: "He went beyond the Jordan River near the place where John was first baptizing and stayed there awhile" (John 10:40).

My response: Father, I see that before the crucifixion, Jesus again goes to the wilderness. Like at the very beginning of His ministry after His baptism, Jesus spent 40 days alone and was tempted. Now, three years later, He's back again and "stayed for a while." Lord, thank You for showing me this "bookending" of Jesus' public ministry. We need wilderness times—quiet times—to strengthen and prepare us for ministry. When I am sidelined for a season, help me to receive it. You have a purpose in all You allow.

"Those who love their life in this world will lose it. Those who care nothing for their life in this world will keep it for eternity."

— JOHN 12:25 —

WEEK SIX

John 11:1-32

Request: Thank You, Lord, for this sacred time to be together. Help me to learn from You today so I am better equipped to be Your child and representative out in the world. In Jesus' Name, I ask this. Amen.

Read: John 11:1-32

Record: Write down one verse from this passage that stood out to you.

Respond: Write a short prayer, talking to God about that verse.

*I*t turns out that Jesus and His disciples did not have a very long time in the wilderness after all, did they? His dear friend Lazarus was ill, and his sisters wanted Jesus to come quickly to heal him. But, as is so often the case, God's plans were different from theirs. Jesus was about to do something so startling and so obviously miraculous that people would be faced with a stark choice: to believe—or to disregard a huge sign of divinity.

I love the way both sisters felt free to speak frankly with the Lord. They just knew that if He had arrived more quickly their brother would not have died. We sense the agony in their voices as they tried to grasp why on earth He had delayed, especially knowing how dearly He loved them. Wisely, though, both of them came to Jesus with their frustrations although Martha came

more quickly than Mary. Oh, let's always speak our hearts to the Savior, shall we? He wants that kind of intimacy with us, and only the truth sets us free after all. When we are hurt or confused or disappointed, it is more than okay to voice that to God. In fact, it's the best thing we can do.

Martha had the great privilege of hearing another "I am" statement from Jesus. All of these statements are stunning and powerful. None of these statements ought to be said by any "nice teachers." Only God can say, "*I am the resurrection and the life. Anyone who believes in me will live, even after dying. Everyone who lives in me and believes in me will never ever die . . .*'" (vv. 25-26). We normal humans have no right nor cause to say such a thing. Wow and wow. To those who had ears to hear, Jesus' declaration of His Messiahship and divinity was clear. John wants us to hear that and makes a point of sharing many, if not all, the occasions on which Jesus spoke as only God has the right to speak.

Today, we leave the story in the middle. Mary has just had her moment at Jesus' feet, weeping because He had not arrived in time to heal her beloved brother. Let's reflect on two applications.

First, God always has a plan, even when we don't understand it. Oftentimes, He works in mysterious ways and not in the specific ways we ask in our prayers. We need to trust Him in those times. Second, when we are distraught or confused by His seeming lack of response or care, still the only place to go is toward Him. We are free to talk to Him at any time . . . for any length of time . . . about anything. He cares. He hears. He comforts. And sometimes, He even helps us understand. All the time, He assures us of His love, and His love we can trust even when we cannot understand.

My verse: "'Everyone who lives in me and believes in me will never ever die. Do you believe this, Martha?'" (John 11:26).

My response: Do I believe this? What an astounding truth! When my body stops, I won't cease to exist. I won't die with it. I'll pass through to eternity with You, Lord! My spirit released—ready to be clothed in a new, immortal body. Death has, indeed, lost its sting. Hallelujah!

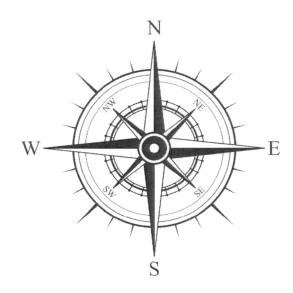

John 11:33-57

Request: I worship You today, Lord. You are the Resurrection and the Life. How grateful I am that I belong to You. Teach me, please. I am here to listen. In Your Name, Amen.

Read: John 11:33-57

Record: Write down one verse from this passage that stood out to you.

Respond: Write a short prayer, talking to God about that verse.

_____

_____

_____

_____

_____

_____

_____

_____

So today, we sit back and marvel. A man dead four days walked out of a tomb and had to be unwrapped from his grave clothes. Many people saw him and did believe. Others went and told the Pharisees. People make very different choices when confronted with Jesus, don't they? Lazarus' story is definitely one I want to hear in Heaven! How did he feel coming back after four days away from Earth—and back into the heavy weight of an earthly body in a fallen world? He was entrusted with a lot, this friend of Jesus. Wow and wow.

I'd love to ponder for a moment Jesus' intense response to this death. He looked around at weeping people, and John tells us he was deeply troubled. In fact, some translations and some commentaries say the word used for deeply troubled is closely associated with anger. *The Holman Christian Standard Bible* says it this way: "When Jesus saw her crying, and the Jews who had come with her crying, He was angry in His spirit and deeply moved" (John 11:33 CSB). And then? After that deep and troubled emotion, He wept. He grieved for this fallen world and the horror of death. And perhaps He grieved over far more that I am not yet wise enough to understand. When God took on flesh, He chose to take on emotions, and that meant He felt anger, sorrow, betrayal, and hurt as well as happiness, peace, and joy. Jesus knows what it's like to hurt. To grieve. **He knows**. And that thought comforts me when I go to Him in distress. This is not theoretical. He wore skin and felt human emotion. He gets it.

So where does Jesus go after this? Back to the wilderness for a few more days. It's almost time for His great sacrifice, but not quite yet. He is going to be the ultimate Passover Lamb, so His death must come at Passover. So, back to the relative quiet of the wilderness He goes and waits for what He knows is to come. What a story of resolve and love. How grateful I am for all He did and felt and taught! These are precious words, aren't they? John, the disciple Jesus loved, has much to share and to add to the first three gospels and this important story is a key addition to the record of Jesus' life.

My verse: "As a result [of Jewish leaders plotting His death], Jesus stopped his public ministry among the people and left Jerusalem. He went to a place near the wilderness, to the village of Ephraim, and stayed there with his disciples" (John 11:54).

My response: Lord, as You move toward Your own Passover death, I love that You stayed in a quiet place during the wait. Except for Your visit to bring Lazarus to life, it's fascinating to me that You chose solitude—no more crowds until Passover. How difficult those days must have been for You as You faced off with death and brought Lazarus back, knowing Your own death— and greater fight—was coming very soon! So many layers are unfolding here. Thank You for taking the road to Calvary for me.

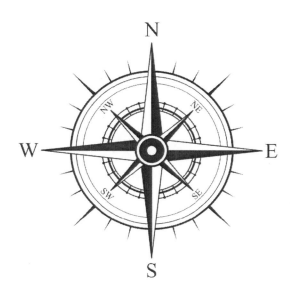

John 12:1-26

Request: Dear Lord Jesus, as I start to walk down the last few days of Your life before Your crucifixion, help me to see clearly all the details John so carefully recorded under the inspiration of Your Spirit. Speak, Lord. Your child is listening. In Your Name, Amen.

Read: John 12:1-26

Record: Write down one verse from this passage that stood out to you.

Respond: Write a short prayer, talking to God about that verse.

_____

_____

_____

_____

_____

_____

_____

_____

*J*oday's reading has three distinct sections. Let's look briefly at each one. First, we attend a dinner, where Mary of Bethany does an astounding thing, pouring a jar of expensive perfume on Jesus' feet. Judas declared the perfume, made from nard, was worth a year's wages. (I just looked up the median income for persons living in the United States based on the 2020 census, and it was $67,521.) So, the equivalent of more than $67,000 just poured out on Jesus' feet! Now that's costly. When we realize this astonishing fact, the lavishness of her gift is magnified. Bible experts say the size of the jar of nard was about the size of a Coke can. It also has a distinct aroma, and like most essential oils, seeps into the skin. It's possible that a faint scent remained on Jesus' skin, and that He was able to sense it during His Good Friday ordeal of beatings and crucifixion. Wouldn't that have been a gift? Jesus loved what she did. He received that extravagance and praised her. She went all out to prepare Him for His burial. She was listening as Jesus talked, wasn't she?

Second, we come to the triumphal entry into the city of Jerusalem. For years, I didn't realize that Lazarus' return from the dead was a big reason the crowds were so large, lining that path on the way to the city. By riding a donkey, Jesus fulfilled a prophecy that most would have known from Zechariah 9:9. "Rejoice, O people of Zion! Shout in triumph, O people of Jerusalem! Look, your king is coming to you. He is righteous and victorious, yet he is humble, riding on a donkey—riding on a donkey's colt." And, of course, as with any parade, more and more people joined in just because it became the thing to do.
Palm branches waving and spirits high, the crowd shouted their praise and temporary adoration. Some were sincere. Others were just having fun and following the crowd. It must have been an awesome sight to witness!

Third, we have a unique situation with some men from Greece. They happened to be in the city, and most commentators believe they were Gentile converts to Judaism. So. They aren't Jewish. They ask permission from Philip, one of the disciples, to see Jesus, and His response to their request is fascinating. I've puzzled over it. He did not say either "sure, bring them over" or "no time for them today." It seems as if He didn't answer the question at all, doesn't it? But I think He did. His mind was on the sacrifice ahead and on that "other flock" He had mentioned back in John 10. He was not only dying for the Jewish people. He was dying for the world. That includes these Greeks and so many more. So, He talks about the harvest that comes from one tiny seed stuffed into the ground. From that seed emerges a plant with many seeds. Jesus will be that seed, willing to die and be buried for the harvest that will come from His sacrifice. These Greeks will be included. How wonderful is that?

My verse: "'I tell you the truth, unless a kernel of wheat is planted in the soil and dies, it remains alone. But its death will produce many new kernels—a plentiful harvest of new lives'" (John 12:24).

My response: The illustration is so clear and understandable in every century and in every culture. Seeds are everywhere. We're dependent on plants for life. And right in the midst of Earth's environment, seen on every inhabited continent, nestles this great truth: Like seeds, when we are willing to die and lose our self-centeredness, You "resurrect" us to new purpose, and many souls are touched and saved in that harvest. I've always loved this verse, Lord.

John 12:27-50

Request: Dear Lord, thank You for the gift of Your death which yielded the harvest of many souls saved and on their way to eternity with You. I am one of them, Lord. It's astounding. I'm here, Lord, ready to learn. Please teach me today. In Your Name, Jesus. Amen.

Read: John 12:27-50

Record: Write down one verse from this passage that stood out to you.

Respond: Write a short prayer, talking to God about that verse.

_____

_____

_____

_____

_____

_____

_____

*T*oday, we read the rest of Jesus' words after the request from the Greek men who wanted to talk to Him. It's an intimate look into His heart, isn't it? He's already dreading the ordeal to come, but willing. He knows this is His Father's will. And Jesus always does His Father's will. As should we. He warns the people who are listening to turn to Him while there is still time.

It's fascinating to me how the response to His message differs. He's clearly stated over the past three years that He is the Son of Man and God's own Son. He's declared Himself to be Light and Bread and that those who turn to Him will never die. He's healed and mended and even raised from the dead. John the Baptist named Him the "Lamb of God" way back at the beginning. The signs surely are there as are His words. Some believe. Some do not.

I love the references to Isaiah. John writes that Isaiah "saw the future and spoke of the Messiah's glory" (v. 41). What must it have been like to be a prophet, to step ahead in time and see Jesus before He was even conceived in Mary's womb? Was it like watching a movie? Was it like looking at a  kaleidoscope? Did God tell Isaiah details as the story unfolded? I don't know, but how strange and wonderful that the prophets were allowed glimpses of Messiah in advance to bring hope and endurance and encouragement to God's people. Isaiah correctly predicted that some would believe and some would not. It seems that after a certain point, if people willfully blind themselves to the truth, God allows that to be a permanent condition. At least, I think that is what is being taught in the verses from Isaiah that John quotes. So, so sad when we block out truth for a lie. May that never be so for you and me!

I was moved by Jesus' agony over what lay ahead, both for Himself and also the agony He felt for those who would not believe. He did not come to judge sinners. He came to save them. But He did declare that those who rejected Him would not be saved. "'I will not judge those who hear me but don't obey me, for I have come to save the world and not to judge it. But all who reject me and my message will be judged on the day of judgment by the truth I have spoken'" (vv. 47-48).

This means that the very worst thing a person can do is to reject the message of salvation. We all sin, and God hates sin. But that He can forgive. The one thing He will not do is to force someone who rejects Him to love Him and choose Him. Pray for those you love who don't know the Lord, that they will turn to Him. He so dearly loves them—and wants them too. Jesus urges people to turn. After all, as He tells the crowd in this passage, "I have come to save the world" (v. 47) and that means—everyone who comes to Him. That's a whole lot of love!!

My verses: "'I will not judge those who hear me but don't obey me, for I have come to save the world and not to judge it. But all who reject me and my message will be judged on the day of judgment by the truth I have spoken'" (John 12:47-48).

My response: This fascinates me, Lord. The worst choice we can make is to reject You and Your offer of forgiveness and eternal life. The best, the greatest choice, is to love You and come toward You and trust You. It is only those who turn away and refuse Your beautiful invitation to life who are judged and condemned. Truly, we all choose our own fate. Lord, I choose You. I choose eternal life. Help me to always run toward You in love and trust. Thank You that You see me through the good times and the hard times . . . then comes Heaven and eternity with You!

John 13:1-17

Request: Heavenly Father, it's so good to know You want me near. Please help my mind to grasp what You want to show me, today. In Jesus' Name, Amen.

Read: John 13:1-17

Record: Write down one verse from this passage that stood out to you.

Respond: Write a short prayer, talking to God about that verse.

*S*cholars believe that John had read the other gospels before he wrote his gospel. If so, he would have realized that some of the key events in Jesus' life had not been recorded. This is especially apparent in the next five chapters. Oftentimes, when something especially traumatic happens to us, the event is more searingly present in our memories. This seems to be the case with John, who recalls that last night before the arrest in vivid detail. He's taken us fairly rapidly through three years of minis-try. Now time slows, and John zooms in on the details, giving us priceless memories of Jesus' last words. These five chapters are a treasure given to us by John. God wanted this part of His story told. Let's listen deeply.

A whole lot happens on Passover night. John sets us up for this section by reminding us that Jesus knew His time had come because Passover had arrived, the time of His offering of Himself for us. He also reminds us that Jesus was fully in control. He knew Judas was going to betray Him. He knew "he had come from God and was returning to God" (v. 3). He knew who He was and was confident in His coming purpose. This is important to note before we read what Jesus does. Jesus Christ, Son of God, Messiah, stoops and scrubs the dirt off His disciples' feet. Our human thinking is that someone low on the social ladder ought to do that job. Someone "less than" should be assigned it. Jesus turns that around totally when He does this job. He who is "more than" anyone ever was. God. Washing feet like the lowest of servants.

I think this shocked His disciples. And I suspect it shamed them a wee bit. None of them had volunteered for that smelly job. Yet it really needed to be done before sitting down together for such a high and holy meal. Jesus didn't scold them. He just showed by example that if there's a job to do, no matter how lowly, one should do it. Jesus made holy the wearisome, ugly but nec-essary jobs of life when He, as fully God, washed feet. In fact, when Peter protested, thinking it highly inappropriate, Jesus insisted.

I recently came across a beautiful way of looking at this foot-washing from another perspective. What if, in addition to the obvious lesson that we should serve others humbly as Jesus served that night, the foot-washing were also a parable of sorts? When Jesus told His disciples that they would understand this more fully later, perhaps this was part of what that phrase meant. John writes that Jesus knew "He had come from God and was returning to God, so . . . "(vv. 3-4). He got up from the table (showing He had left heaven); He took off His robe (in a few hours He would be stripped and humiliated); He washed the disciples' feet (His death would wash away their sins); He put His robe back on (He would rise from the dead); He resumed His seat at the table (He would take—and has now taken—His rightful seat at God's right hand in His Kingdom). Perhaps this was a beautiful acted-out story that the disciples would not understand now, but someday would (v. 7). I love this thought, and it wouldn't surprise me at all if God was communicating this as well as the more obvious application.

Let's return to the practical as we close out these thoughts. Jesus makes a point of telling the disciples that they should also be in the business of washing feet. What does that look like today, do you think? I think it means caring for an aging parent when some of the tasks might be unpleasant. It means helping a friend who is injured by offering to do her laundry and change her kids' diapers. It means helping clean up after a church dinner. It means being willing to get our hands good and dirty in order to serve someone else who has a genuine need. Jesus vividly illustrated this, didn't He? Let's go and do likewise and remember Him as we do.

My verse: "'And since I, your Lord and Teacher, have washed your feet, you ought to wash each other's feet'" (John 13:14).

My response: Lord, You came to serve. And if I am to follow You, that means I too am to serve. Help me to have a willing heart to do the "ick" jobs. How beautifully You showed us the dignity in stooping low to help others.

"So now I am giving you a new commandment: Love each other. Just as I have loved you, you should love each other."

— JOHN 13:34 —

WEEK SEVEN

John 13:18-38

Request: Lord Jesus, I am humbled by Your willingness to wash dirty feet. You are Lord of all. King of kings. Yet You serve those You love. Make me more like You, and please teach me today as I read Your Word. In Your Name, I pray, Amen.

Read: John 13:18-38

Record: Write down one verse from this passage that stood out to you.

Respond: Write a short prayer, talking to God about that verse.

ow we enter into a section of the Bible that shows us the deep suffering of Jesus in the realm of relationships. Jesus understands the hurt of betrayal and denial. He chose to be human in every way and that meant feeling the pain and distress of loving those who turned on Him. If you've ever been betrayed by someone close to you or been left in the dust by a friend you thought would stick by you, be comforted. Jesus knows the unique sting and stab to the heart when one you trust behaves in horrible ways. Let's walk through Jesus' experience by looking first at Judas and then at Peter.

John lets us see Jesus' emotions in the latter part of chapter 13. He has just bent down as a servant and scrubbed filthy feet clean. And He did not skip Judas' feet. He washed and cleansed  them as well. Knowing that Judas was about to betray Him, hurt. Broke His heart. Judas had not only witnessed all the miracles and heard all the sermons and stories Jesus told, but he'd also performed miracles in Jesus' Name when he was sent out with all the disciples, two by two, to visit towns and villages and share the good news. Judas had been entrusted with handling all the donated money, given by good people to further Jesus' work and ministry. Jesus loved Judas. And Judas chose to steal and betray that love and trust.

I suspect Jesus' ache was not just the betrayal. He ached for all Judas would lose through his actions. Judas certainly regretted his decision soon after he made it. It brought him no happiness or joy. Matthew tells us that Judas did not last long after his betrayal: "When Judas, who had betrayed him, realized that Jesus had been condemned to die, he was filled with remorse. So he took the thirty pieces of silver back to the leading priests and the elders. 'I have sinned,' he declared, 'for I have betrayed an innocent man.' 'What do we care?' they retorted.

'That's your problem.' Then Judas threw the silver coins down in the Temple and went out and hanged himself" (Matthew 27:3-5). Remorse is a horrible companion. If you've ever been betrayed, feel assured that you can run to Jesus, knowing He understands uniquely and personally the trauma you feel. Ask for strength to pray for your betrayer.

Jesus also knows in advance that Peter will deny even knowing Him. He knows that Peter won't stand up for Him or defend Him at all. Peter will duck and hide and lie rather than be associated with the Lord during His trial. And yet . . . with all these hurts . . . Jesus breaks bread and pours the cup and loves on His disciples. John does not repeat the words Jesus spoke about the bread representing His body and the  wine representing His blood as the other three gospels do. He shares what was not told before. The point to notice here is Jesus' deep love for them. Despite knowing they will all desert Him in His time of need, He loves them and speaks with them and shares truths with them.

One command stands out at the end of this chapter. Jesus urgently tells His disciples to love each other. He says, "'Your love for one another will prove to the world that you are my disciples'" (v. 35). Isn't that the truth? When we love radically, like He does, washing the feet of those who betray us and teaching life lessons to those who will desert us . . . we are noticed

as quite different from the rest. Whenever Christians forgive heinous crimes done against them, the world sits up and takes notice. Jesus loves fully, radically, selflessly. He instructs us to do the same—to which I reply, *"Only with Your help, dear Lord! Only with Your help and by Your grace."*

My verse: "Now Jesus was deeply troubled, and he exclaimed, 'I tell you the truth, one of you will betray me!'" (John 13:21).

My response: Oh, I cannot even imagine the grief, the sorrow, the dread You must have felt that night, Lord. You were no emotionless robot working on autopilot. Although fully God, You were also a fully living, breathing, loving man. Humanity, by its very nature, means feelings and opens itself to hurt, woundedness, and pain. You loved Your disciples. You hurt when Judas betrayed You, and verse 33 makes me think You grieved leaving the others as well. Lord, it's a bit beyond me, how You could be human and divine—but thank You that You loved us and hurt for us.

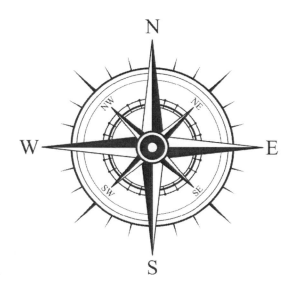

John 14:1-14

Request: Father God, Your child is here, eager to hear from You. Please teach me today. In Jesus' Name, Amen.

Read: John 14:1-14

Record: Write down one verse from this passage that stood out to you.

Respond: Write a short prayer, talking to God about that verse.

_____

_____

_____

_____

_____

_____

_____

_____

I love how Jesus continues His talk with these confused disciples. Knowing that He will soon be betrayed and captured, Jesus has just said goodbye to Judas. He simply shook His head at Peter's bravado, knowing it wouldn't last. One might imagine that Jesus would be a little self-absorbed at this point. He is about to die after all. But not our Lord Jesus. Instead, He's concerned about His disciples. He reaches out to them with words of comfort. "Don't let your hearts be troubled" (v. 1), He says. He's leaving them, yes, but, oh, the place He is preparing in Heaven for them! If only they could see all that lies ahead for them in eternity! Hebrews 12:2 says that Jesus endured the cross because of the "joy set before Him," and we see that play out right here. He's already designing their special places in His mind!

This reassurance is cut a bit short, first by Thomas and then by Philip. They have no idea where Jesus is going or how to get there—and, by the way, could He explain better His relationship to His Father? From these questions come some great and beautiful words. Jesus declares, *"I am the Way, the Truth, and the Life"* (v. 6). We need to look to Him and trust that He will lead us home. He is all we need. I love the simplicity. Like a sheep with a Good Shepherd, I just need to follow and trust. He also declares that He and the Father are one. Our doctrine of the Trinity was formed partially from these very verses. Jesus is God in flesh. Huge, crazy, and beyond our understanding, yet true. God distilled Himself in flesh as Jesus, yet remained in Heaven as the Father, and eventually, after Jesus died and rose again, sent Himself as Spirit to live within His followers. It's a magnificent, marvelous mystery.

Don't you love that Thomas and Philip are not afraid to ask questions? What does that tell us about Jesus and His approachability? To me, it says that I can ask questions too. He'll answer them and not brush me off. And I do ask Him . . . often. I love coming to Him with everything, knowing He listens and cares and will make clear to me those issues that feel murky. Even if, like the disciples, it takes me a while to understand.

Sometimes, when I'm by myself, I love to think about the special place being prepared for me. What will it look like? How stunning to think that Jesus was excited about getting ready for us to join Him in Heaven! Just like I put fresh water and mints and even a little present beside the guestroom bed for my guests to tell them how glad I am they've arrived . . . Jesus is waiting for us to join Him. He's preparing for that. He loves us that much. And I just bet, knowing God's endless creativity, that each of us will have a space awaiting individually crafted, unique and precious to us.

My verse: "Jesus replied, 'Have I been with you all this time, Philip, and yet you still don't know who I am? Anyone who has seen me has seen the Father! So why are you asking me to show him to you?'" (John 14:9).

My response: Philip's head must have been spinning. The mystery of the Trinity is great. Thank You, Holy God, for revealing Yourself to us in human flesh. This gracious gift is a rich one. Priceless.

John 14:15-31

Request: Dear Father, I'm so thankful You call me to come to You. Here I am. Please show me truths from Your Word, today. In Jesus' Name, Amen.

Read: John 14:15-31

Record: Write down one verse from this passage that stood out to you.

Respond: Write a short prayer, talking to God about that verse.

_____

_____

_____

_____

_____

_____

_____

_____

*T*he very first verse in this section is an important one for us to study. Jesus declares that if we love Him, we will obey Him. Now there's a test. Do I love Jesus? Well, how willing am I to do what He says? Do I forgive others as He asks me to? Am I willing to pray for my enemies? Do I seek His Kingdom first? These are hard commands. And yet, over the years, I have seen that when I follow them, life goes so much more smoothly, and it brings joy to my Heavenly Father as well. I show Him I love Him by listening carefully to what He says and pleasing Him by doing it.

This passage also tells us quite a lot about the third member of the Trinity—the Holy Spirit. God's Spirit is omnipresent. He can be in all places at all times. In Psalm 139, David describes it this way:

> *I can never escape from your Spirit! I can never get away from your presence! If I go up to heaven, you are there; if I go down to the grave, you are there. If I ride the wings of the morning, if I dwell by the farthest oceans, even there your hand will guide me, and your strength will support me. I could ask the darkness to hide me and the light around me to become night—but even in darkness I cannot hide from you . . .. —Psalm 139:7-12a*

Our God can literally indwell us. He can live in each one of us individually and whisper to us from within. What a tremendous gift and honor His children are given! Just as God the Father spoke to Jesus on Earth, and Jesus moved in accordance with His Father's will at all times, so can we. There's no greater joy than listening to the One who made us and knows best how we ought to live, especially because He loves us and wants the best for us in light of eternity.

At the close of this chapter, Jesus talks about the Spirit that resides within, God Himself, who brings peace to our hearts. We don't need to be troubled because God is with us and in us. Always. "Don't worry," Jesus is saying to His disciples. "All will be well. I will still be with you in

a unique and powerful way." He then ends this part of the conversation, and they begin moving from the upper room to the garden of Gethsemane. Jesus still has more to say as they walk. Oh, how thankful I am that John recorded these amazing last words of Christ to His beloved disciples. They are rich with truth and meaning.

My verse: "'But I will do what the Father requires of me, so that the world will know that I love the Father. Come, let's be going'" (John 14:31).

My response: Love is preeminent in the story of Your death and resurrection. First, we're told God so loved the world that He sent You, Lord Jesus! And here Your love is affirmed. No matter how Your humanness recoiled from the death to come, Your love for the Father compelled You onward. The mystery of all this is beyond me, Lord God. But I am deeply grateful that You are love and that You act in love toward me.

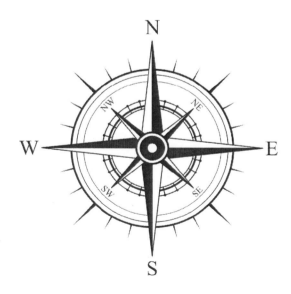

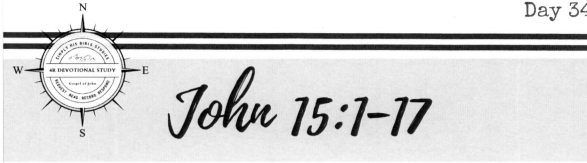

John 15:1-17

Request: Dear Lord, how I thank You that You are everywhere. Here with me and even within me by Your Spirit. Please give me clear thinking and a softened heart as I read Your Word today. Thank You. In Jesus' Name, Amen.

Read: John 15:1-17

Record: Write down one verse from this passage that stood out to you.

Respond: Write a short prayer, talking to God about that verse.

*I*remember living in Stuttgart, Germany, when my husband was in the military. One of our favorite walks was through a nearby vineyard etched into the side of a hill with row upon row of grapevines. It stunned me to see the harshness of the pruning each year. The stubs that were left looked unable to produce anything ever again. And yet, spring would come and branches would spring up, leaves would unfurl and grapes would glisten in the late summer sun. What a process!

I wonder if Jesus and His disciples were walking by a vineyard when He spoke to them, preparing them for the pruning and the fruit-bearing to come. They go together, you see—pruning and fruit-bearing. His disciples were going to face much opposition and tragedy in the years ahead. At the same time, they would see miracles beyond imagining and thousands of people choosing Christ despite threats of persecution as the Church grew and flourished. I suspect that the principles of the vine and the branches steadied them and grounded them as they fulfilled His calling on their lives.

If we want to bear fruit—and that is our job—we need to pay attention to this analogy. Over and over, Jesus uses the word "abide" or "remain" in His directives. I like the translations that use the word abide best of all. To abide is to move in with someone and live with them. It is to stay with them. A branch can't wander away from its vine, can it? It has to stay firmly attached, one with the vine and the roots, so it can produce grapes. That's the way it must be with us. We need to stay so close to the Lord at all times. Some mornings I wake up and even whisper that word to myself. "Abide." *Oh, Lord, today help me abide with You, do life with You, all day long with no separation between us.*

I love knowing our mission. "I appointed you to go and produce lasting fruit," says Jesus in verse 16. I do want to leave a lasting legacy behind me, don't you? The Bible describes fruit in different ways. Jesus talks about good works being fruit in Matthew and Paul shares that the Spirit living within us produces character fruit like love, joy, and peace. And then, of course, the harvest is plentiful, and we are to go and gather fruit/souls and bring them to the Lord who can save them. Fruit that lasts is fruit that will be eternal in some measure.

Over and over, Jesus tells us the way to reach hearts: love others. I counted the number of times the word love was used in today's passage. Nine times. Jesus loves His Father, and He loves us. He commands us to love each other. He tells us this will bring great joy as well as fruit! We can't lecture, bully, or drag people into God's Kingdom. Nope. We are to show them the way by our great and unusual love for them. Just as God draws us with His own great and unusual and undeserved love.

The great strategy for winning people to Christ is simple. Stay attached to God and His love, and then let that love from Him saturate and overflow out of you toward others. That kind of love will attract others to you and to Him, the source of love. We all have different gifts that we use as well, but the preeminent plan is to love God and love others. And for that? We need to abide in Him, close as can be, because He is the very source of the love we crave and that the world needs to see in us.

My verse: "'You didn't choose me. I chose you. I appointed you to go and produce lasting fruit, so that the Father will give you whatever you ask, using my name'" (John 15:16).

My response: The disciples here are reminded of their beginnings. John was fishing with his father when Jesus chose him. How amazing that must have felt to be singled out. And the mission is also ours (because You chose us too, Lord!)—to produce lasting fruit. Oh, Father, help me to work toward that—helping people find their purpose in You—showing others the way to eternal life and walking so closely with You that I know how to pray in Jesus' Name for the things You want here on Earth.

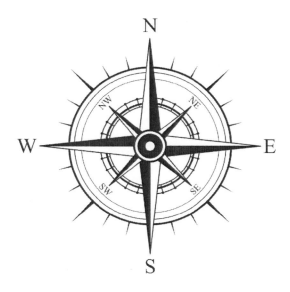

John 15:18-27

Request: Today, Lord Jesus, help me to abide in You. Help me to stay firmly attached, Your obedient branch, soaking up Your love and sharing it with all I meet. And teach me, please, as I open Your Word this morning. In Your Name, I ask this. Amen.

Read: John 15:18-27

Record: Write down one verse from this passage that stood out to you.

Respond: Write a short prayer, talking to God about that verse.

*H*ave you ever been hated because you were a Christian? Has anyone ever mocked you or turned away with a roll of the eyes because of what you believe? If so, take heart at Jesus' words in the second half of John 15. Sometimes, just being a believer is enough to make someone dislike you. Not because you did anything wrong, but because you belong to the Lord, and the person who hates you prefers the darkness to the light. It's comforting to realize that Jesus too was hated. And He did everything perfectly. We sometimes feel that if something bad happens to us, it's our fault. Not always. Sometimes, we make people mad because we've behaved badly. But sometimes our principles make them angry, even if we have shared them correctly.

I remember one of the first times I was actively hated because of my Christian principles. I was a college student, earning my tuition by waiting tables at a steak restaurant in a nearby town. I thought everything was fine between me and my fellow servers. We all seemed to get along, but that all changed the night they discovered I accurately declared all my tips at the end of each evening. This puzzled me. Didn't they tell the truth about how much money they made? That was the rule, after all. The IRS was pretty clear on the form I had to fill out after every shift.

The mood quickly became hostile. I was encircled by a small mob of five women, all berating me at once for my stupidity in correctly declaring my tips. At first, I couldn't understand why this would bother them, but evidently, they were afraid they'd be found out if a tax auditor examined their nightly reports (averaging $10 in tips) and compared them to mine (averaging $50 in tips at that time). Their anger was rooted in fear of being caught. I left work that night a trembling mess of nerves. They were all older than me, and their words were not kind. However, I held to the right way, apologizing that this made life harder for them. (Apologizing felt kind. Oy.) It was a hard season for me and a life lesson in standing up for what's right at personal cost.

Now, of course, what I went through that night pales into insignificance when compared with what believers in nations around the world face from hostile unbelievers. In my lifetime alone, Christians have been speared to death, burned alive with their children, kidnapped, beheaded, and more. Christians in China languish in prison and "re-education camps." Christian villages are attacked and burnt to the ground in some parts of Africa. All simply because they claim the Lord Jesus as their God and King.

I wonder if those words we read today in John 15 bring our persecuted sisters and brothers a measure of comfort. "'Do you remember what I told you? "A slave is not greater than the master." Since they persecuted me, naturally they will persecute you. And if they had listened to me, they would listen to you'" (v. 20). In his letter to the Philippians, Paul yearns to share in the "fellowship of [Jesus'] sufferings" (Philippians 3:10 NKJV). When we realize that our persecution is because we are recognized as His very own, there's a sweetness in the suffering. We experience a fellowship—suffering together with Jesus, part of the same body of which He is the head.

And that leads me to the last reassurance in this chapter. Jesus comforts His disciples after this hard warning. The Holy Spirit is coming and will enable us to testify to the truth of who God is! We often just want the "pretty parts" of Christianity: The comfort God gives, the release from bondage and sin, and the joy of knowing we are going to Heaven. It's important to also realize that the road may be very painful and hard. But Jesus walked it first, and He will be with us through it all.

> "Blessed are those who are persecuted for righteousness' sake, for theirs is the kingdom of heaven. Blessed are you when they revile and persecute you, and say all kinds of evil against you falsely for My sake. Rejoice and be exceedingly glad, for great is your reward in heaven, for so they persecuted the prophets who were before you."
> —Matthew 5:10-12 NKJV

LOVED. A BIBLE STUDY

My verse: "'If the world hates you, remember that it hated me first'" (John 15:18).

My response: Lord, I've lived in a time of very little persecution here in the USA. I am grateful. Help me to remember, though, as the days grow darker, that if I am hated because I'm a Christ-follower . . . they hated You too. And You lived a perfect life. Haters gonna hate. (And help me bear it, Lord! I will need You strongly in such a time as that!)

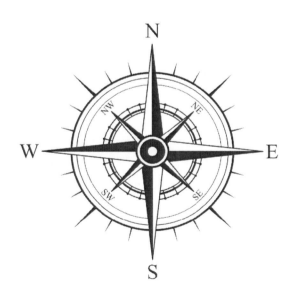

"I have told you all this so that you may have peace in me. Here on earth you will have many trials and sorrows. But take heart, because I have overcome the world."

— JOHN 16:33 —

WEEK EIGHT

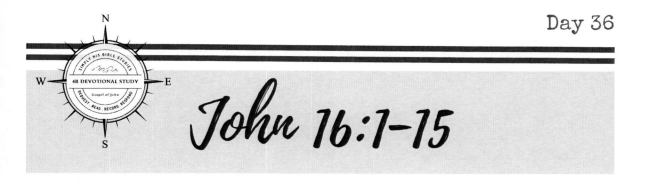

John 16:1-15

Request: I praise You, Lord. You hold out to me words of life every day as I come to You and read Your Word. Speak, Lord. I am listening. In Jesus' Name, Amen.

Read: John 16:1-15

Record: Write down one verse from this passage that stood out to you.

Respond: Write a short prayer, talking to God about that verse.

*O*h, how Jesus loved His disciples. He knew they were going to be headed into the adventure of a lifetime, full of stunning victories and crushing sorrows. In the very first verse of our reading today, Jesus shares the reason He is talking with them so seriously and deeply: "'I have told you these things so that you won't abandon your faith'" (v. 1). There it is. When we know ahead of time that not everyone will agree with our belief system, we will be better equipped to stand against the current in hard situations.

Our faith in a God who loves us is true and right and so very, very good. But to people who do not believe, it can feel very threatening. Not everyone wants to believe that a God exists, who runs the universe and has the sovereign right to tell them how to live. Even if He is good and all of His commands are for their  ultimate good. Many want to go their own ways and make their own foolish decisions. For some unbelievers, being around a Christian, who believes God is in charge, is just not going to sit well. Over and over throughout the centuries, including in our world today, hatred rises up against peaceful Christians who want to share God's love with the world. We need to be ready. Jesus doesn't want us to be shocked when the hard times come.

Oh, but we don't go through these hard times alone! When Jesus returned to Heaven, He sent the Holy Spirit to His followers. The Greek word used for the Holy Spirit in this passage is *Paraclete*. It's an interesting word that has been translated as advocate, counselor, comforter, or encourager. The original and historical meaning of the word "Paraclete" was "called to one's side." I love that. The Spirit of God in the form of the Holy Spirit is called to our side . . . to be with us, advocating, comforting, encouraging, and counseling throughout our days on Earth, whether they be bright and happy or dark and frightening. He doesn't leave us. And since He is included in the Trinity, He knows suffering through what He went through on the cross as Jesus. One God. Manifested in three specific Persons. And the Spirit is with us, called to our side. Hallelujah!

One last thought for today. I am so intrigued by verse 12. Jesus is longing to tell His disciples even more. But He doesn't. "There is so much more I want to tell you, but you can't bear it now," He says. Perhaps even now, when I have no clear explanations for hard questions, the reason is the same: I can't yet bear it. I am not wise enough or far-seeing enough to understand the "why." Job demanded that God give him a reason he had to suffer so terribly. Instead of directly answering and sketching out for Job His entire plan for the universe, God simply revealed to Job . . . Himself . . . in all His creative majesty and glory. And Job shut his mouth. Some things are just too hard for us. We need to be okay with mystery and settle within ourselves that we are children, who are still too young to understand the ways of a good and infinitely wise Father.

My verse: "'There is so much more I want to tell you, but you can't bear it now'" (John 16:12).

My response: That's the way I felt when our daughters went to college—wait! I thought. I have so much more to tell them! But people can only bear and process so much. And the disciples were about to witness a traumatic event: betrayal and crucifixion of the One they loved and followed. Father, You knew how much they could take in. Help me to trust You in what I don't yet understand. Perhaps, I'm not ready to "bear it." I love that You, Lord Jesus, wanted to share and teach Your disciples so many things—and therefore—You want to teach us!

John 16:16-33

Request: Spirit of the Living God, breathe fresh on me. Teach me, show me, stay with me as I study the God-breathed words of the Bible today. In Jesus' Name, Amen.

Read: John 16:16-33

Record: Write down one verse from this passage that stood out to you.

Respond: Write a short prayer, talking to God about that verse.

_____

_____

_____

_____

_____

_____

_____

*J*ust about every mother has a labor and delivery story. No one yawns and says, "My labor was no big deal. Quite boring, actually." Especially when delivering that first baby, labor can be intense and scary and new and also very painful. My first labor lasted over 24 hours. Since I delivered in a teaching hospital, I foolishly gave permission for interns to learn from my labor. Big mistake. It was hard enough without extra people hovering about. In the end, I needed Pitocin, a drug that helped speed up contractions, but then I needed drugs to help me endure the Pitocin. I was basically a wimp. When the drugs took effect and I felt no more pain, I came closer to worshiping a human being (my doctor) than I ever had before or since. The relief was huge.

But then, our baby girl was born. And she was perfect. Tiny, dainty, cutest little nose, and the most beautiful child ever. Of course. I wept tears of joy. I didn't want her out of my arms or out of my sight. I felt a fierce, strong, protective love for her that was new to me. I love my husband dearly, but the particular kind of protective fierceness that overwhelmed me with our baby girl was uniquely new. I was smitten. I couldn't stop staring at her. You see, I had longed for a baby for many years before God blessed us with our Kathryn. I had wept many tears about my childless state. Oh, but my mourning turned to joy with the birth of this child!

Jesus uses the analogy of labor and delivery to describe what is coming for His disciples. They are about to go through intense, unrelenting pain. And, unlike my pain of childbirth, no drugs will take it away. Also unlike mine, their pain will endure more than 24 hours without relief. The darkness of that time must have been horrifying. But then, the news came to them . . . Jesus is alive! Incredibly, the impossible had happened. Jesus Christ, Son of God, Messiah walked out of that grave and brought with Him the gift of eternal life for all who believe and a right to be called children of God. From deepest despair to incredible joy!! What a story.

It's our story too. There are days here on Earth that are hard for us. There are times when all we can do is weep and lament and writhe in pain. Life is hard. But take heart, dear one. Joy does, without a doubt, come in the morning. It all ends well. Jesus leaves us with a beautiful promise and assurance. "'I have told you these things, so that in me you may have peace. In this world you will have trouble. But take heart! I have overcome the world'" (John 16:33 NIV). Take heart! Our Savior and Lord has overcome the world. And we belong to Him.

My verse: "'But the time is coming—indeed it's here now—when you will be scattered, each one going his own way, leaving me alone Yet I am not alone because the Father is with me'" (John 16:32 NIV).

My response: It's hard for me to realize that all these words of advice and preparation were spoken mere hours before Your arrest. I'm so amazed by Your love, Lord! You continued to pour into Your disciples right up to the end, knowing they were all about to scatter and run away, leaving You alone with the soldiers. Yet not alone because Your Father remained with You. As You always remain with me when I feel alone. Oh, how sweet that is.

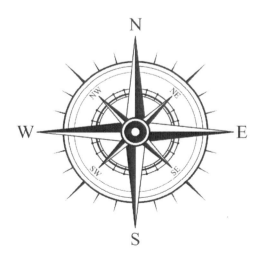

John 17

Request: Father God, thank You for John, the disciple You loved. Help me to read his words about Jesus' last moments on Earth with understanding and eyes to see the richness. I ask it in Jesus' mighty Name, Amen.

Read: John 17

Record: Write down one verse from this passage that stood out to you.

Respond: Write a short prayer, talking to God about that verse.

_____

_____

_____

_____

_____

_____

_____

*W*e now reach the last words of Jesus in this whole discourse He had with His disciples on His way to the Garden of Gethsemane. They were walking out of Jerusalem and down a steep hill to a ravine called the Kidron Valley. Jesus' last words were not to the disciples. They were words of prayer to His Father lifted on behalf of those disciples. Jesus also prays for those who would come to know Him because of the faithful testimony of the disciples—He prays for us! It's important to note that Jesus believed in the importance of prayer and God's power to answer. As He finishes His words of preparation for them, He turns to His Father in prayer for them. Oh, how I love His example for us and His rich, rich prayer.

He starts with a prayer of completion in a sense. He prays that all He does would glorify God. And then, He speaks the reasons for His prayer: to give eternal life to others . . . to help them know the living God . . . to complete the work He was assigned . . . and to finally be brought back to Heaven to share again in the glory of it all. He has completed the assignment and rejoices in that, and He reports verbally to the Father so the disciples can "listen in" and hear His heart.

Next, He prays for these dear disciples that He has loved and labored over for three years. Let's look at a list of what He prayed so we can ponder the richness of His heart for His disciples.

Protect them by the power of God's great Name.

Help them stay united.

Keep them safe from the evil one.

Make them holy by God's truth.

Teach them the word which *is* truth.

He finishes this prayer for them by offering Himself in prayer so that these desires of His heart for them can come to fruition: "And I give myself as a holy sacrifice for them so they can be made holy by your truth'" (v. 19).

Then, He does something amazing. He prays for you and me. Yes, He does! John 17:20 is the pivot point as He turns from prayer for the current followers to the future followers: "'I am praying not only for these disciples but also for all who will ever believe in me through their message.'" Your Lord and Savior specifically prayed for you as He walked toward the Garden of Gethsemane! What He had just prayed for His closest friends, He desires for us as well. Then He lists specific requests for future believers like us. He wants us to be:

Unified—just like Jesus and the Father were united on Earth.

Committed to Christ—abiding so close that the world might believe in God.

Eager to show through our unity that we genuinely love the one true God.

Totally convinced that we are deeply loved.

Welcomed one day to Heaven where we will see God's glory and be with Him forever.

Filled with God's love and God's Spirit dwelling within us.

This. This is what our Lord Jesus wants for each of us. So, next time we feel all petty and irritated when something doesn't go our way at church or with fellow believers, let's remember how He labored in prayer for us, that we would be united in our love for Him and united in showing the world His love!

My verse: "'Now, Father, bring me into the glory we shared before the world began'" (John 17:5).

My response: Jesus is homesick for Heaven! What a beautiful prayer! Lord, I love the yearning You express—and allow us to hear. You are about to be sacrificed on behalf of all people, but You are looking beyond that to being back in the glory of Heaven. Thank You, Lord Jesus, for this glimpse into Your heart!

John 18:1-24

Request: Lord, I am overwhelmed that You, on the night You were betrayed, prayed for . . . me! I turn to You now during this time set apart to be with You. Teach me, please. In Jesus' Name, Amen.

Read: John 18:1-24

Record: Write down one verse from this passage that stood out to you.

Respond: Write a short prayer, talking to God about that verse.

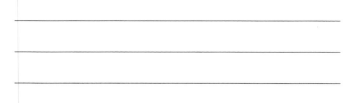

*I*cannot imagine how painful it must have been for John to remember what happened next, right after Jesus' prayers for His dear ones. I love that John shares these amazing prayers. However, in his narrative, he does not include the agonizing prayers Jesus prayed in the Garden of Gethsemane, asking if there could be any other way. We read about those in Matthew, Mark, and Luke. Do you see how beautiful it is that we have all four gospels? Each one adds to the whole in God-inspired ways.

The details of that night are so vivid. John remembers the frightening arrival of the soldiers led by Judas "with blazing torches, lanterns and weapons" (v. 3). Later, at the high priest's home, John remembers the cold of the night and the warmth of the charcoal fire. In between, he can still see Peter slicing off the ear of Malchus. What a confusing, horrible, terrifying kaleidoscope of memories must have crowded his mind as he sat there writing, asking the Spirit to show him what details his account should mention.

John kindly does not report that most of the disciples fled. We learn that from the other gospel writers. He also does not brag that he's the one who knew the high priest and was able to gain admittance for Peter into that courtyard with him. He lets us know what happened, but in great humility, not drawing attention to himself. The fact remains, however, that John was loyal. He was there. As close to Jesus as he could be under the circumstances. He was able to hear many of the conversations with Jesus that night. I suspect also that knowing the high priest and his household gave John inside information on those conversations.

The long night begins for Jesus with this arrest. His first stop is the house of Annas, the father-in-law of the then-current high priest, Caiaphas. Annas had also been a high priest in the past. He and Caiaphas were among the most powerful Jewish religious leaders of that time. Jesus is asked questions to which Annas already knows the answers. When Jesus points that out, a guard slaps

Him across the face. The physical abuse of Jesus has begun. He's already experienced the mental torment of facing the cross back in the Garden of Gethsemane. Now He offers His body on our behalf and submits to literal torture, beginning with that slap.

When Annas cannot draw out anything satisfactory from Jesus, he sends Him on to his son-in-law, the current high priest. They try to trick Jesus into speaking blasphemy so they can show the people how horrible He is.

One more thing to notice. Jesus never loses His calm during this arrest and forthcoming ordeal. Luke tells us in his gospel that He fixes Malchus' ear in the garden after telling Peter to put away his sword. "' . . . Shall I not drink from the cup of suffering the Father has given me?'" He asks Peter (v. 11). Jesus is ready to suffer. Watch Him as we continue reading tomorrow, and He continues to be dragged from place to place. The suffering grows more intense, but the calm remains. God strengthens Him to be ready and willing to sacrifice Himself on our behalf. Glory be His Name!

My verse: "But Jesus said to Peter, 'Put your sword back in its sheath. Shall I not drink from the cup of suffering the Father has given me?'" (John 18:11).

My response: Peter was prepared to fight for You. The harder work of submitting to injustice and dying a martyr's death was still beyond him—so he denied knowing You. To willingly endure death rather than deny Your Name, Lord, is a whole different kind of hard than fighting back. Help me to be willing, if such a time should come to me. (. . . but I'd much rather be spared. As would we all!)

John 18:25-40

Request: Heavenly Father, equip me to do Your will today in every encounter and every circumstance. In Jesus' Name, Amen.

Read: John 18:25-40

Record: Write down one verse from this passage that stood out to you.

Respond: Write a short prayer, talking to God about that verse.

_____

_____

_____

_____

              _____

              _____

              _____

              _____

*T*his section contains Peter's second and third denials of Christ, predicted earlier in John 13:38. It was evidently easier for Peter to take up a sword and fight for Jesus than to admit he was a follower of Jesus, especially in a situation that could easily get him arrested and probably killed alongside Jesus. Peter was a fighter and Jesus was not fighting. Isaiah tells us that Jesus went like a lamb to the slaughter. Later, we will see the redemption of our Peter. John devotes just a few verses to the story of the denials. He'll invest more words in telling of Peter's restoration. I love that about John. He tells the whole truth, even the ugly parts, but he speaks longest on the beautiful parts!

However, right now we are in a horrible part of the story. Jesus is up all night and is still at Caiaphas' house early in the morning hours. Next, He is brought to Pilate, the Roman governor. Jesus has a fascinating exchange with Pilate. It's almost as if He sees in Pilate one who might be searching for truth. How cool would it be when we get to Heaven to find out that Pilate had repented and was saved? Who knows? With God all things are possible, and Pilate was obviously struck by Jesus' demeanor and calm.

Very few people, I am sure, had ever stood before this Roman governor, who had the power to crucify them . . . and calmly talked about truth. But Jesus does. Jesus even talks about His Kingdom. He assures Pilate that it is "not of this world," He's not planning a rebellion. Nevertheless, He does have a Kingdom and that makes Him a King. He tells Pilate that He has come into our world to tell us the truth. And He did! He told us how God loved us so much that He sent Jesus to pay the penalty for our sins. Now, He doesn't say all of that to Pilate as far as we know, but He came to Earth to tell that story and live it out for sure and certain.

One of the hardest parts of this story comes at the end of chapter 18. Pilate is not convinced that Jesus is a danger to Rome or harmful in any way. He wants to release Jesus. So, to celebrate their high holiday of Passover, he offers them Jesus as their released prisoner. The other alternative is a revolutionary named Barabbas. And the crowd shouts out in favor of Barabbas. Oh, crowds are fickle, aren't they? Just a few days ago, Jesus entered Jerusalem with a huge crowd dancing in front of Him, waving palm branches, amazed at the resurrection of Lazarus. And now, a crowd shouts out for His death.

Let's be careful about this in our own lives. Going along with the momentum of a crowd passionate about a cause is much easier than refusing to go along. The emotions that come when people cling to a "great cause" or scream at a "terrible injustice" make it very, very hard to oppose them in a way that will be heard. But we can't be influenced by crowds. A whole lot of people passionately believing an untruth does not change the fact that it is untrue. We need to be unmoved by the crowd, firmly grounded in truth. That is what Jesus came to share with us after all. The truth.

My verse: "Jesus replied, 'Is this your own question, or did others tell you about me?'" (John 18:34).

My response: Okay, so first of all, how many humans on trial for their lives start asking the judge or authority figure their own questions? Second, this question fascinates me. Did You see in Pilate a sheep from another fold? Someone who had a little bit of a seeking heart? And, Lord, I wonder if historians know whether or not Pilate received You as Lord and Savior. I hope he did. It's a mystery. But I love that You asked Pilate this question. You cared about him—this official who thought he was in control—this human that You Yourself had formed and made.

But these are written so that you may continue to believe that Jesus is the Messiah, the Son of God, and that by believing in him you will have life by the power of his name.

— JOHN 20:31 —

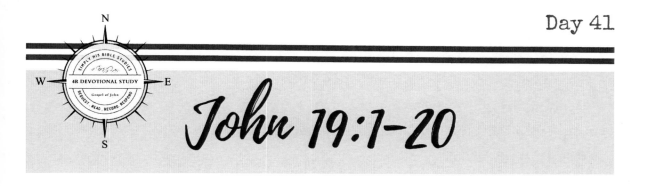

John 19:1-20

Request: Dear Father, thank You for Your love for me. Keep me close to Your heart, Lord, and help me to live wisely today. In Jesus' Name, Amen.

Read: John 19:1-20

Record: Write down one verse from this passage that stood out to you.

Respond: Write a short prayer, talking to God about that verse.

_____

_____

_____

_____

                    _____

                    _____

                    _____

                    _____

*H*ave you ever been mocked and abused? Thankfully, it's not a common occurrence for most of us. I do remember an incident in elementary school that has stuck with me all these years. As in any school, we had the "in" crowd, the popular kids—and the kids who were not. One day, a girl, who desperately wanted to be a part of the "in" crowd, talked to me on the walk home, mourning her fate. In my bossy and superior way, I dismissed all those kids out of hand and told her they were all uninteresting as human beings and had no minds of their own. They had to walk in lockstep with each other, always afraid they'd wear the wrong outfit or say something that made them less cool. I thought I was being an encouragement to her. Looking back, I was not being kind. I lumped all the popular kids together in my silly disdain without knowing any of them. Each of them had unique personalities, but I was too young and too full of justifications about why I liked being an outsider to realize that.

In any case, this girl told that crowd what I had said. As a result, I had the most miserable recess of my life. Four or five of the popular girls mocked me, yelled at me, kicked me, and chased me away from wherever I tried to just sit and be still on that playground. They were relentless, and they were furious. It was pretty awful. Their actions did nothing to change my opinion of them, and it was no fun to be abused like that. I realize now that I had hurt them. And people who are hurt often hurt back. Back then? I just wanted the recess bell to ring and save me.

That little incident was horrifying to my sixth-grade self. And yet, I had participated in the sinfulness of it by my disdain. Jesus was without sin. He was King of all creation, and He allowed His creatures to mock Him, spit on Him, and torture Him. I shake my head in wonder.

We continue to see Pilate trying to save Jesus. Jesus' "crime" of claiming He was the Son of God did not seem worthy of crucifixion to Pilate. He tried hard to back out, but that mob was relentless, and Pilate could have no rest until he agreed.

They reminded him that Jesus had declared Himself a king, letting Pilate know that if he didn't authorize the crucifixion, they'd be sure the Romans in charge knew he had tolerated a threat to Caesar. Not true, but it could have been messy for Pilate. So. He caved.

But, don't you love the sign he designed for Jesus? In John 19:19, we read the words, written in three different languages: "Jesus of Nazareth, the King of the Jews." Our Lord died with the truth written out in Greek, Hebrew, and Latin above His head. Oh, the irony. Oh, the sorrow. It hurts me to even think about Jesus on the cross. The shame of nakedness, the wounds from the lashes, the crown of thorns. The ever-increasing difficulty Jesus would have had pushing against nails to lift Himself enough to breathe, slowly suffocating. It's all too much. And yet this is what He chose to do to save us from our sins by taking the punishment upon Himself. May we never, ever get over the awe and sorrow of this pivotal moment in time.

My verse: "Then Jesus said, 'You would have no power over me at all unless it were given to you from above. So the one who handed me over to you has the greater sin'" (John 19:11).

My response: All power is Yours, Lord Jesus. Help me to remember that when powerful leaders of today scare me. If they wield power now it is only because You have allowed it for this season. And thank You also for this reminder that You see the hearts of people. You saw that the greater sin was not Pilate's but those who brought You to Pilate. Thank You that You alone judge correctly. You alone hold the power. And You alone chose to restrain Yourself that long ago day in order to save us.

John 19:21-42

Request: Oh, how grateful I am for all You did on my behalf, Lord Jesus! Help me to see with fresh eyes today as I read of Your crucifixion. I bow my head in gratitude. In Your Name, Amen.

Read: John 19:21-42

Record: Write down one verse from this passage that stood out to you.

Respond: Write a short prayer, talking to God about that verse.

_____

_____

_____

_____

_____

_____

_____

_____

*a*nd now we come to the moment in history when God made right all that was broken by the fall of humankind in the Garden of Eden. Justice was satisfied in the death of Jesus, and His subsequent resurrection confirms it. Today we are focusing on His last moments and His death. One of the stunning truths in this passage is that so much of what occurs had been seen centuries before by various prophets. Let's look at some of these amazing prophecies and marvel.

His Clothing

So they said, "Rather than tearing it apart, let's throw dice for it." This fulfilled the Scripture that says, "They divided my garments among themselves and threw dice for my clothing." So that is what they did. —John 19:24

They divide my garments among themselves and throw dice for my clothing. —Psalm 22:18

The Sour Wine

Jesus knew that his mission was now finished, and to fulfill Scripture he said, "I am thirsty." A jar of sour wine was sitting there, so they soaked a sponge in it, put it on a hyssop branch, and held it up to his lips. —John 19:28-29

. . . they offer me sour wine for my thirst. —Psalm 69:21b

His Bones

So the soldiers came and broke the legs of the two men crucified with Jesus. But when they came to Jesus, they saw that he was already dead, so they didn't break his legs. —John 19:32-33

"Each Passover lamb must be eaten in one house. Do not carry any of its meat outside, and do not break any of its bones." —Exodus 12:46

The Pierced Side

One of the soldiers, however, pierced his side with a spear, and immediately blood and water flowed out. —John 19:34

" . . . They will look on me whom they have pierced and mourn for him as for an only son. They will grieve bitterly for him as for a firstborn son who has died." — Zechariah 12:10b

Isn't this astounding? John thought so. Over and over as he shares the details of the crucifixion, he refers to scriptures that prophesied these details hundreds of years beforehand. I can't even begin to imagine the thrill of discovery for John and all of Christ's followers as they read familiar passages in what we call the Old Testament and realized they had been fulfilled before their very eyes. What a wonderful affirmation to them that Jesus was indeed the long-awaited Messiah. Detail after detail lined up with the words of God written long ago.

Another example is Jesus' burial. Joseph of Arimathea and Nicodemus were both prominent and wealthy men, who before the crucifixion had been followers of Jesus, but in secret due to pressure from their peers, the religious elites. Now, they step forward and give Jesus a proper burial, complete with all the expensive spices placed between the layers of the grave clothes.

Jesus' body is not dumped in a pauper's grave. It's reverently laid in a new tomb, never-before used. The prophet Isaiah wrote about this long ago. At the time, his prophecy must have seemed impossible. Here is what he said: "He had done no wrong and had never deceived anyone. But he was buried like a criminal; he was put in a rich man's grave" (Isaiah 53:9). Now, how could that be true? Why would an innocent man be buried like a criminal? Why would someone who was thought of as a criminal be given a rich man's burial? And yet, as we know, that is exactly what happened to Jesus. Though He had done no wrong, He died a death reserved for criminals. And He was buried in a rich man's tomb. All the details. All the signs. Throughout John's gospel, we see the clear truth he wishes us to know. Jesus was God in the flesh, promised Rescuer of His people—and the people of the whole world. He died so we could live. He loved us all that much.

Last little thought for today. How honored John must have felt at the cross to be singled out as the caregiver for Mary, Jesus' amazing mother. What a statement of trust that was when Jesus told John and Mary that they were to be linked together. I am sure that blessed John richly. No wonder he felt confident in declaring himself to be "the disciple whom Jesus loved." We never hear if the other disciples were at the cross. They might have been. Or perhaps not. We know this. John was there. He was there when Jesus was tried, and he was there when Jesus was taken down from the cross. John loved Jesus that much.

My verse: "And he said to this disciple, 'Here is your mother.' And from then on this disciple took her into his home" (John 19:27).

My response: I have so many questions, Lord. Why did You choose John to watch over Mary and not one of her own children or relatives? Had Mary grown close to John and the disciples by following Jesus with them? Was Mary's wisdom needed in the early church so that it was best for her to live with John and near the disciples? What sort of home did John have? I'm left with the sweetness of this, though. John was trusted with the care of Your precious mama. And Mary evidently stayed with John until her death. Oh, so many stories yet to be heard when I reach Heaven!

John 20:1-18

Request: Dear Father, I am grateful for a new day in which I have the joy of meeting with You and learning more from Your Word about the best event in all of history. Give me eyes to see this story unfold in technicolor today, Lord! I am ready. In Jesus' Name, Amen.

Read: John 20:1-18

Record: Write down one verse from this passage that stood out to you.

Respond: Write a short prayer, talking to God about that verse.

_____

_____

_____

_____

_____

_____

_____

*J*ohn devotes a lot of time here to Mary Magdalene. And well he should. Mary was the first one at the tomb as soon as the Sabbath was over. She was the first to let everyone know the body had disappeared. And then, she was the first to see and speak with Jesus. She was given the huge joy of shouting the news: He is alive! Can you even begin to imagine this? Oh, the puzzlement at first! Could it be true? Oh, the churning of emotions from despair to pure, unadulterated, wild, expansive, explosive *Joy*!! The unimaginable had happened. Jesus had conquered death and walked out of that grave. Hallelujah!

Let's talk about the grave clothes for a moment. John mentions them in some detail, and I think that is significant. The way I understand it, they weren't "unwrapped" and lying scattered about as if someone had taken them off of Jesus. (Remember Lazarus when he came out of the tomb? Someone had to unwind miles of grave-cloth strips to free him.) Jesus' body just came out of them and left them lying there. Jesus was fully human, but He was still able to do  pretty amazing things with His body. Even before His crucifixion, He walked on water. After the resurrection, Jesus was able to pass through objects like grave clothes and walls and doors. He appeared and disappeared at will. When He simply exited His grave clothes, John tells us He even folded the face cloth and left it tidily in a separate place. Another sort of signal that He was done with death. It was finished. Once and for all.

I'd like to chuckle at something with you. I find it most amusing that John, who, so far, has been quite humble and reticent about himself, did find it necessary to point out that he won the foot race with Peter and arrived at the gravesite first. I think that's typical for childhood friends, right? John beat Peter in the race to the tomb. It's another detail that makes me confident his story is true. Who but John would remember that little detail and feel we ought to know it?

I am not sure Peter was alive by the time John finished writing his gospel. If he was, and he read that part, I bet his eyes rolled.

The last part of this section makes me tearfully glad. Our Mary Magdalene, who loved the Lord so very much, was given the privilege of seeing Him! I love that it was His voice that helped her recognize Him. At first, she had no idea who was standing near her by the tomb. She surely did not think it was Jesus. She was determined to find His body. I am sure her eyes were swollen with tears, so it's no wonder she didn't realize who it was. And it's clear she wasn't fully looking at Him because John tells us that when Jesus tenderly said her name, she turned to Him. The awe and astonishment must have been immense. I suspect she was trembling like a leaf. Overcome with emotion, right? From darkest despair to incredulous hope to buoyant joy. That's exhausting. But in the nicest possible way.

Jesus had warned the disciples that their experience would be like childbirth. Intense labor and pain followed by joy in the morning. Let's read that word from Him again. "'I tell you the truth, you will weep and mourn over what is going to happen to me, but the world will rejoice. You will grieve, but your grief will suddenly turn to wonderful joy. It will be like a woman suffering the

pains of labor. When her child is born, her anguish gives way to joy because she has brought a new baby into the world. So you have sorrow now, but I will see you again; then you will rejoice, and no one can rob you of that joy'" (John 16:20-22). How amazingly accurate His prophetic words were. I'm not surprised. He is, after all, the omniscient, all-knowing God. I just love how this story ends! But more is still to come.

I'm so glad you've taken this journey with me, entering into John's memories, led by the Spirit. What riches we have unearthed together aided by that same Spirit alive and in us today.

My verse: "Mary Magdalene found the disciples and told them, 'I have seen the Lord!' Then she gave them his message" (John 20:18).

My response: Father, You honored women with this choice of Mary Magdalene in such a special way! Eve, the first woman, was deceived and saw sin enter the world. Sin bit deep. Her firstborn son killed her second born. And now, a woman who had been inhabited by demons, a result of the fallen world that came about from paradise lost in the Garden of Eden, is honored to be the one to see You first and deliver Your message. Not only is Your body gone from the tomb—You are here on Earth, walking around and giving messages. The gladdest of words, "I have seen the Lord!"

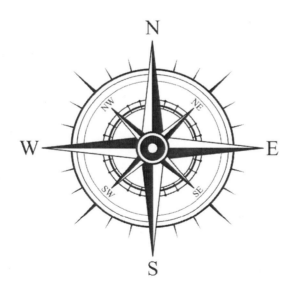

John 20:19-31

Request: Dear Lord, I come to You in this quiet moment, asking for wisdom and understanding as I read further about Your resurrection from the dead. Teach me, please, as I read. In Jesus' Name, Amen.

Read: John 20:19-31

Record: Write down one verse from this passage that stood out to you.

Respond: Write a short prayer, talking to God about that verse.

_____

_____

_____

_____

_____

_____

_____

I love this portion of the story. It tells the disciples' very real struggle believing that Jesus had physically risen from the dead. He wasn't a ghost. And even if His body seemed able to walk through doors and grave clothes, it was still His body. The wounds were still visible, could be felt and touched. No, Jesus was not a ghost. Jesus was not someone else pretending. Jesus was Jesus, come back from the dead. You and I would have struggled too. It's hard to believe the miraculous. I suspect that is why Jesus lingered on Earth before He went back to His Father in Heaven. His followers needed to be sure of the reality of His resurrection beyond a shadow of a doubt. They did not know yet that one day they would lay down their own lives based on that sure knowledge that He truly did come back from the dead.

Thomas, in particular, was a hard sell. He wasn't with them the first time Jesus appeared and pretty much refused to believe the accounts of his trusted friends. He would have to see for himself. And not just see—he wanted to touch those wounded hands and put his hand on the  pierced side. Without that kind of proof? Thomas wasn't buying it. And then Jesus was there! Entering a locked room once more and directly appealing to Thomas in His patient, loving way. Come touch. Come feel. Believe. I love Thomas' very succinct response: "My Lord and my God!" (v. 28). Thomas was all in from that moment. Church tradition tells us that he was killed in India by jealous Hindu priests. Once Thomas saw Jesus? He never wavered. To and through a martyr's death. And then, of course, his own resurrection into Heaven.

We now return to verses we looked at in the introduction to this study, verses that state John's reason for writing his gospel. Right after Thomas' declaration, John makes one of his own. "The disciples saw Jesus do many other miraculous signs in addition to the ones recorded in this book. But these are written so that you may continue to believe that Jesus is the Messiah, the Son of God, and that by believing in him you will have life by the power of his name" (vv. 30-31). John was writing to Christians who had watched thousands of their brothers and sisters in Christ die martyrs' deaths. Christians were used as human torches to light the way to the coliseums where other Christians were torn to bits by lions as entertainment. John is encouraging them that they are right to continue believing that Jesus is indeed the Messiah, the Son of God. John assures them that they will have life by the power of His Name.

Jesus had lovingly shown Thomas the scars on His hands and side, but He tells Thomas, "... 'You believe because you have seen me. Blessed are those who believe without seeing me'" (v. 29). That's you. That's me. That's my husband, Ray.

Ray was an atheist when I met him. I tried my hardest to convert him to Christianity. I wanted him saved, not only for his own sake but because I really liked him and did not date non-Christians. (Yes, I am confessing to an ulterior motive.) Ray has a Ph.D. in history. Even back in high school, he loved history. What convinced my skeptic to accept Christ wholeheartedly? The deaths of the apostles. His logical mind could see no other explanation for their willingness to die than that they truly had seen a dead man return from the grave. I'm so thankful for their testimony that still points to the truth today: Jesus is the Messiah, the Son of God.

My verse: "Eight days later the disciples were together again, and this time Thomas was with them. The doors were locked; but suddenly, as before, Jesus was standing among them. 'Peace be with you,' he said" (John 20:26).

My response: Lord, I am puzzled at the eight-day gap. Where were You when You weren't with Your disciples? Your resurrected body could obviously appear in various places. Where did You go? I am so thankful, in any case, that You were patient with Thomas, showing him Your wounds, and I am in awe of the mystery of Your resurrected days on Earth.

John 21

Request: Thank You, Lord, for this time of study in John. Help me remember the lessons You've taught me. Show me what to study next, and teach me today, please, more truth from this great book. I ask in Jesus' Name, Amen.

Read: John 21

Record: Write down one verse from this passage that stood out to you.

Respond: Write a short prayer, talking to God about that verse.

_____

_____

_____

_____

_____

_____

_____

Well, here we are. The very last chapter in the Book of John. As is typical of John, we read an account of a day not mentioned in the other gospels. John doesn't end with Jesus' ascension back into Heaven and His last words to His disciples. Instead, he chooses to tell us one more important moment that, led by the Spirit, he knows we need to hear. As John says in his very last words in his book, "Jesus also did many other things. If they were all written down, I suppose the whole world could not contain the books that would be written" (v. 25).

This story, though, was important enough to be included. (Doesn't it make you wonder about all the stories left untold? I can't wait to hear some of them in Heaven someday!)

I love that Jesus meets His disciples fishing again. Fishing was John's whole identity when he first met Jesus. His father, Zebedee, owned a fishing business, and he and James, his older brother, would have inherited it. Instead, of course, the brothers left their dad and followed the Lord. So, we come full circle at the closing of this gospel. They're fishing and failing. Again. Jesus tells them to cast the net on the other side, and it fills with 153 large fish (I love that John remembered the exact number—and that the net was not torn!) Is it foreshadowing all the people they will "catch" as they form the early church? Maybe . . .

Again, a charcoal fire is burning on the shore. We last saw Peter standing by a charcoal fire in the high priest's courtyard, denying he knew Jesus. This time, Jesus feeds him and the others and then restores Peter with a thrice-asked question, "Do you love me?" Peter is given the opportunity to affirm his love out loud. What a blessing that must have been. I am fascinated by Jesus' responses, to feed His sheep. The cost will be high. Does Peter love Jesus enough to spend his life telling others of the Shepherd and eventually lose that life as a martyr? He does. And he did. Church tradition tells us that Peter, like Jesus, was killed by crucifixion. Peter was distressed, but only because he did not feel worthy to die as

Jesus had died. So he asked to be crucified upside down. Redeemed by Jesus, Peter had a chance to prove his loyalty a second time and did not fail. I love that God gives us second chances, don't you? And third chances . . . and more! We are blessed to be given fresh starts as often as we come back to Him in repentance.

John also takes this time to clear up a misconception. By the time he wrote this gospel, he had outlasted most of the original followers of Jesus. Jesus had told Peter not to worry about what was going to happen to John. That was John's story. From that had come a rumor that John would never die, but this was not true. John  clarifies that Jesus was simply telling Peter to stick to his own story and not worry about John's. According to church tradition, though, John was hard to kill. He'd even been placed in boiling oil and survived it and then was banished to the Isle of Patmos. He did eventually die and was finally reunited with the Savior who loved him. All his life, John knew he was loved. That knowledge fueled him for the work God had given him, including writing this amazing account of the life of Christ told by the "one Jesus loved." Our John.

How about you? Can you smile and shyly say, *I am the one Jesus loves*? You are, you know. He loved you enough to put on flesh and die for you. He loves you enough to want you to come near every day, hearing His voice through the Bible and through the quiet that comes in prayer times. Like Peter, we sometimes wonder about other people's stories. From the outside looking in, perhaps we even think we'd like their story better than our own. But that's the wrong perspective. Your story is precious and rich and unique to you. I hope that as you have read this gospel with me over these weeks, you've heard from the living God and have seen more of His plan for you unfold. I hope that most of all, you know that you are indeed . . . *Loved.*

My verse: "Jesus repeated the question: 'Simon son of John, do you love me?' 'Yes Lord,' Peter said, 'you know I love you.' 'Then take care of my sheep,' Jesus said" (John 21:16).

My response: I've always looked at this in the past as Peter's restoration service after his three denials, and it is. But today, Lord, I see in this Your intense love for people who do not yet know You or who are just learning. If we love You—we can show our love by caring for the sheep. Not just feeding ourselves and being glad we're saved. What blesses You, Lord? When we care for the sheep. That's how important Your great commission was to ". . . 'Go into all the world and preach the gospel to every creature'" (Mark 16:15b NKJV). Each little lamb is of great worth to You. Help me to be willing to serve, to go after the lost, and to strengthen the flock all the days of my life. Because I love You, Lord. And I truly feel . . .

Loved.

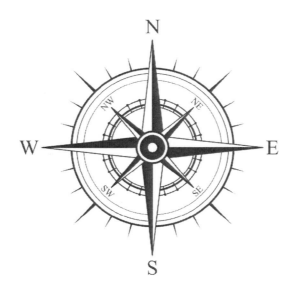

"For this is how God loved the world: He gave his one and only Son, so that everyone who believes in him will not perish but have eternal life."

— JOHN 3:16 —

G R O U P   S T U D Y

Optional Group Study

Digging deeper into . . .

Loved.

A Bible Study of the Gospel of John

Dear Group Members: The goal of the book you are holding is that you, the reader, will meet with God individually, trust Him to show you truths from His Word, and spend time pondering what He teaches you. I want so much for you to experience the joy of daily time alone with Him, hearing from His Spirit as you study His Word with a listening heart. A group study is optional. This guide is for small groups who choose to band together to share and study further. These are not homework questions to add to your daily study. The questions in this guide are to be seen and studied in a group setting. Hopefully, they will help grow your understanding of the passage while joining together in prayer and growing as believers. I envision members helping each other through sharing and further study. May God bless your group times mightily!

Dear Group Leaders: Your most important job as a leader is to pray for the group ahead of time. Ask the Lord to give you His wisdom and discernment, and then rely on His Spirit to lead and guide during the group time. The weekly lessons are designed to help you shepherd your group toward greater understanding of the passage and also toward life changes. My heart's desire is that group meetings will be rich times of sharing and strengthening each other through fresh Bible reading, accountability, and prayer. God created us to be part of His body, growing honestly through life's trials and helping one another along the way. Please don't feel you have to "finish" the questions each week. Feel free to linger over questions when a need is felt. Your primary goal each week is to address the needs of your unique group. May God guide you as you love on each member and learn right along with them how much we are . . . loved.

You are loved,
Sharon

Sharon Gamble, author

Introductory Meeting

Group Leader Notes

1. Open in prayer. Ask God to lead your study; ask that His Presence will be felt, and His Name lifted high.

2. If members are buying their own books, remind them before meeting time to bring them. If you or your church has purchased the books, pass them out at this introductory meeting.

3. Spend some time getting to know each other.

4. Read the book's introduction out loud together.

5. Lead the group in a discussion of the introduction. What did they find intriguing?

Quiet Time (10-12 Minutes)

Have group members read Psalm 139 silently a couple of times and ponder these words that explain the special place each one has in God's heart.

1. Choose a favorite verse from Psalm 139 to share with the group, and write it out here:

2. Go around the circle and share your verse. If it's not too personal, we'd love to know why you selected this verse. How did God speak to you through it?

Group Discussion

Take another look at John 20:30-31 together. Have someone read it out loud, and answer these questions.

1. Why do you think John wanted people to know that he had not recorded all the signs and miracles of Jesus?

2. The New Living Translation chooses to highlight the verb tense used for "believe" in this passage—"continue to believe." The Amplified Version translates that word as "believe [with a deep, abiding trust]," and the New International Version adds the footnote that "believe" can also be translated as "continue to believe." So here's the question: Why did John choose a word that can mean both to believe and to continue in belief as part of his reason for writing about Jesus' life on earth?

3. Talk together about the heart of John's intention in writing this book. What exactly does he want us to believe after reading his gospel?

Assignment for the Coming Week

1. Read Days 1 – 5 this week.

2. Make sure you write out your verse and response each day.

3. Review all five days and choose the day and verse that stood out to you most. Come prepared to share that verse with your class next week.

What about the other two days of the week?

We want you to read the Word every day, not just five days a week. Here are some suggestions for the other two days:

1. Reread the chapters in John included in the week's assignment and write a short reflection about the passage as a whole.

2. Read one Psalm on your sixth day and one and a half chapters in Proverbs on the seventh day. For most, these will be your weekend days.

3. Choose and enjoy a devotional book that incorporates Scripture. (*Sweet Selah Moments: Encouragement for Daily Living*, Sharon's first book, would be a good choice.)

Note: Each week at this group time, after you share your favorite verse of the week, you will work as a class to answer various questions together about the previous week's devotionals. You are not expected to have answers to group discussion questions prepared in advance. Your focus during the week should be to meet with God each day, discover "your verse," and write your response. The group study questions are to be answered as a group when you are together.

Close in prayer.

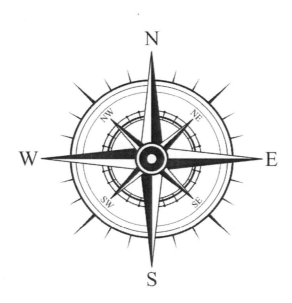

Week One Group Study

Open in prayer.

1. Start by sharing with each other a favorite verse from your readings this past week. Talk about why it "mattered" to you and, if willing, share your response to the Lord about the verse.

2. Read aloud John 1:1-18. Create a list of all you learn about Jesus from these verses.

3. Why do you think John started at the very beginning of time in his gospel?

4. John the Baptist is mentioned in both chapters 1 and 2. What do you learn about his character from John the disciple?

5. In what ways do you wish to be more like either John the Baptist or John the disciple? And why do you value that part of their character?

6. What are some practical ways we can make sure our conversations are not all about us, but also about our love relationship with God? How do we change the way we talk about Him depending on who we are with—nonbeliever, interested inquirer, or follower of Christ?

7. Many people feel a little uncomfortable with the way Jesus spoke to his mother when she asked Him to help. How about you? Why do you think He answered as He did?

8. Sharon thought that perhaps Mary didn't know what Jesus was going to do, but rested in knowing that Jesus would do what was right. Do you think this is a plausible possibility? What else could Mary have been thinking?

9. Bible scholars disagree about when and how many times Jesus cleared the temple. Most conservative scholars believe Jesus cleared it twice. Once at the beginning of His ministry as John tells us in chapter two and once near the very end of His ministry. If you have time left, compare the accounts of the clearing of the temple. Read these passages out loud and then discuss how they are similar and how they are different. Do you agree that Jesus most likely cleared the Temple two times? Why or why not?

   Matthew 21:12-13   Mark 11:15-17   Luke 19:45-46   John 2:13-22

10. John points out something interesting about Jesus and His knowledge of human nature at the very end of chapter two. Despite the fact that many people started believing in Jesus due to the miraculous signs, Jesus wasn't convinced they were all genuine followers. Reread John 2:23-25 and discuss what Jesus said. How does one discern who really believes and who is just along for the show?

Assignment for the coming week: Read Days 6 – 10, and write out your verse and response each day. For your two "days off" when you won't be reading new material in John, choose one of the activities listed in the Introductory Meeting assignment. Come prepared to share a verse and response.

Close in prayer.

Open in Prayer.

1. Start by sharing with each other a favorite verse from your readings this past week. Talk about why it "mattered" to you and, if willing, share your response to the Lord about the verse.

2. Read together John 3:1-20. Why was Nicodemus confused by what Jesus said? List the verses that would have been hard to understand, and try to summarize, as a group, Jesus' main message to Nicodemus.

3. Why do you think Jesus answered Nicodemus the way He did with illustrations and a whole new way of thinking?

4. Let's look at John the Baptist together. Read Luke 1:5-17 and Matthew 3:1-17. What do you learn about this specially chosen man?

5. Unlike the prophet Jonah, who was chosen by God and ran as fast as he could in the other direction, it looks like John the Baptist embraced his calling fully. What are the benefits of just doing what God says? Why is it often so hard for us to simply obey?

6. John the Baptist always rejoiced when Jesus was honored. How can we have that mindset today in our everyday life?

7. The woman at the well was a social outcast in her day. Who are the social outcasts in our day? How do we reach out to them? What is the value in knowing someone's story, like Jesus knew hers? How do we facilitate people sharing their stories?

8. Do you have a person in your life who is a good listener, hearing your story and then pointing you toward truth? Share with the others and learn from godly examples.

9. Sharon talks about prayer and receiving answers to prayers that don't always align with our wills. Have you had a time in your life when God seemed silent or did not answer the way you wished He had?

10. What helps you continue coming to God, even knowing He is not your "magic genie" standing ready to obey your wishes?

Assignment for the coming week: Read Days 11 – 15, and write out your verse and response each day. For your two "days off" when you won't be reading new material in John, choose one of the activities listed in the Introductory Meeting assignment. Come prepared to share a verse and response.

Close in prayer.

Open in Prayer.

1. Start by sharing with each other a favorite verse from your readings this past week. Talk about why it "mattered" to you and, if willing, share your response to the Lord about the verse.

2. This week, you read the first of seven "I AM" statements Jesus declares and John reports in his gospel. Read John 6:32-40 together. Then, read Exodus 16:11-36. What stood out to you about bread and manna in these accounts?

3. Bread is a common food item found in most cultures. Perhaps that's one reason Jesus chose it to represent who He was to the people. Why do you think He declared Himself the "Bread of Life"? What is it about bread that might teach us more about who Jesus is?

4. Manna wasn't bread as we know it. In fact, its very name means "What is it?" Yet, God calls it "bread" in Exodus 16:12b: " . . . and in the morning you will have all the bread you want. Then you will know that I am the LORD your God." From the verses about manna you read, what do you learn about God and Jesus, who called Himself bread?

5. Jesus spoke uniquely to the man who was lame. He asked if he wanted to be well, and he also warned him to stop sinning. Is it possible that the man was so "used to" being lame that Jesus questioned him about whether he really wanted to be healed? What other reasons might Jesus have had for asking that question?

6. The Jewish leaders were quite strict about keeping the Sabbath. They even had rules against carrying things around because they felt that was "work." Why do you think they created the rules? Do you think they lost the heart of keeping the Sabbath by doing so?

7. Read Exodus 20:8-11 for more details on this Sabbath command. How can we honor God's command to rest without the command itself becoming a burden and not at all "restful"?

8. In John 6, we read about Jesus having quite the busy day feeding hordes of people and walking across a storm-tossed lake after fending off a crowd that wanted to force Him to be king. What do you learn from Him about handling hard situations?

9. What prevents you from finding peace in stormy times? What helps you regain that peace?

10. How are you doing at finding daily time to meet with God? What's hard about it? Share what your time each day looks like. Can you encourage those who are struggling with this? It's not easy, and the enemy of our souls definitely tries to interfere with our time of stillness with God. Take time to pray for each other.

Assignment for the coming week: Read Days 16 – 20, and write out your verse and response each day. Choose one of the activities listed in the Introductory Meeting assignment for your two "days off." Come prepared to share a verse and response.

Close in prayer.

Week Four Group Study

Open in Prayer.

1. Start by sharing with each other a favorite verse from your readings this past week. Talk about why it "mattered" to you and, if willing, share your response to the Lord about the verse.

2. Read aloud together Genesis 1:1-19 and Revelation 21:22-27.

3. What was created first, vegetation or the sun?

4. What was created first, light or the sun?

5. What source of light is used in Revelation 21 to light the city? Discuss what this means: God is more Light than the sun is light.

6. Jesus is gaining in popularity, and the religious leaders don't like it. Compare and contrast what it would be like to be a Jewish leader at that time as opposed to an average Jewish layman. How were their interests aligned? And how were their interests different? Why do you think it was easier for the "regular people" to believe than it was for many of the leaders to believe? What stumbling blocks today prevent people from believing?

7. Talk about shame together. Recall the story of the woman caught in adultery and reread John 8:32. Sharon suggests that one of our freedoms as Christians is freedom from guilt and shame. Why do you think that is hard to believe for many people?

8. Jesus told people to eat His flesh and drink His blood in John 6:53-58. Did you struggle with this passage? What conclusions did you reach about Jesus' meaning?

9. In John 7, we discover that Jesus' brothers don't yet really believe He's Messiah. Do you think this is typical of siblings? Have you seen rocky sibling relationships with misunderstandings? How did Jesus handle their urging to go "prove Yourself"? What can you learn from that for your own life?

10. Jesus declares again that He is living water. At this point, He has compared Himself to bread, water, and light. What do these elements have in common, and why do you think He chose them to help people know Him better?

Assignment for the coming week: Read Days 21 – 25, and write out your verse and response each day. Choose one of the activities listed in the Introductory Meeting assignment for your two "days off." Come prepared to share a verse and response.

Close in prayer.

Week Five Group Study

Open in Prayer.

1. Start by sharing with each other a favorite verse from your readings this past week. Talk about why it "mattered" to you and, if willing, share your response to the Lord about the verse.

2. Read aloud together Psalm 23 and Ezekiel 34. Both of these passages are full of references to sheep and shepherds and in some key ways they are parallel passages to John 10, where Jesus declares Himself to be the Good Shepherd. As you read, make a list together of characteristics of a good shepherd. Discuss bad shepherds, too. In Ezekiel, God is angry with the leaders of His people. They are doing a terrible job of tending the flock. As we care for children or others under our care, what can we learn from these passages so that we are good shepherds emulating the Best Shepherd?

3. In John 8, Jesus calls the devil a murderer and a liar. In fact, He calls the devil the "father of lies." When we know this, we can be on guard against lies. Can you name some lies you have believed that were not true?

4. Why do you think Jesus healed several times on the Sabbath, the day on which the religious leaders of that time considered it forbidden "work"?

5. Why do you think the blind man was not healed instantly but had to go wash mud from his eyes? (If you have time, check out together the story of Naaman in the Old Testament together in 2 Kings 5:1-19. Do you see similarities?)

6. The blind man was brave and spoke what he believed to be true about Jesus. This cost him his right to worship in the synagogue, which was the heart of community in his culture. How can we be ready, like him, to risk derision if placed in a similar situation where telling the truth is going to "hurt" us?

7. Peter, a close friend of our John, faced a challenge along with the other disciples when they were told to stop speaking about Jesus. Their answer, in Acts 5:29, was simple: "We must obey God rather than man." Can you think of any examples in our world, today, where people have had to make similar choices?

8. Jesus and His disciples end up back in the wilderness near where John the Baptist first preached. Why do you think that was where Jesus chose to go in these last quiet days before Passover and His crucifixion?

9. Talk about wilderness moments together. Why are there so many in the Bible? What do you think were the reasons Jesus withdrew to that wilderness? Have you ever withdrawn like that for a season? How did it shape you?

Assignment for the coming week: Read Days 26 – 30, and write out your verse and response each day. Choose one of the activities listed in the Introductory Meeting assignment for your two "days off." Come prepared to share a verse and response.

Close in prayer.

Week Six Group Study

Open in Prayer.

1. Start by sharing with each other a favorite verse from your readings this past week. Talk about why it "mattered" to you and, if willing, share your response to the Lord about the verse.

2. Read aloud together Luke 10:38-42. This is the other time in the gospels that Mary and Martha are mentioned. What added insights do you learn about the sisters from this passage? Talk about their different temperaments for a moment and how both were loved by Jesus. Are you more like Martha . . . or Mary? Both women have good points, even if Mary usually gets most of the praise!

3. Read aloud together Luke 7:11-17, the story of Jesus restoring a young man from death. Lazarus was the second man Jesus raised from the dead. Compare and contrast these two occasions of miraculous resurrections by Jesus. How are they alike? How are they different? What do you learn about Jesus from these accounts?

4. Martha and Mary were both disappointed in Jesus when He didn't arrive quickly to heal Lazarus. What can you learn from the way they handled disappointment?

5. Just moments before Lazarus was called back to life, Jesus wept at Lazarus' tomb. The Bible also says Jesus was angry. It's a strong word. Here are some synonyms from various commentaries that help you see the depth and force of this word: deeply troubled; vehement agitation; a painful, sympathetic, and shuddering movement;

a snort; strong moral indignation and wrath. What do you think was the reason for Jesus' strong reaction?

6. Have you ever been swept up in a great and holy moment with a huge crowd of people, similar to those waving palm branches as Jesus entered Jerusalem? Describe what it was like. What's good about worship and awe in a large group? What are the dangers of feeling that amazing surge of awe along with other people and then . . . returning to folding laundry and cleaning bathrooms?

7. Talk about Mary's lavish gift of pure nard poured out on Jesus' feet. Why was this so significant?

8. Discuss the concept of a seed having to "die" in order to bear fruit. In what ways have you had to die to self in order to honor the Lord?

9. John 13 gives us a unique peek into the Upper Room where Jesus and His disciples met for the Passover. What did you think about the idea that Jesus was enacting a parable with the foot-washing, showing what was about to take place? Does that give insight into His statements: You won't understand this now but you will later? And, if you don't let me wash your feet, you can have nothing to do with me?

10. Share with each other what tasks feel like "washing smelly feet" for you. How have you managed to serve in hard ways? How has God helped you? What do you learn about servant leadership in this passage?

Assignment for the coming week: Read Days 31 – 35, and write out your verse and response each day. Choose one of the activities listed in the Introductory Meeting assignment for your two "days off." Come prepared to share a verse and response.

Close in prayer.

Week Seven Group Study

Open in Prayer.

1. Start by sharing with each other a favorite verse from your readings this past week. Talk about why it "mattered" to you and, if willing, share your response to the Lord about the verse.

2. Read Psalm 31 out loud as a group. What do you learn from David about prayer during times of persecution? Do you see ways that Jesus might have identified with this psalm as He prepared to suffer for our sakes?

3. Talk about how Jesus treated Judas at this last supper together, despite knowing Judas would betray Him. How can we be like Jesus in the way we treat those who are unkind to us?

4. John mentions himself in chapter 13 verse 23: "The disciple Jesus loved was sitting next to Jesus at the table." Why do you think John calls himself this, instead of sharing his name? What significance do you think there is in where he was sitting?

5. One of the most controversial verses in the Bible is John 14:13. "You can ask for anything in my name, and I will do it, so that the Son can bring glory to the Father." Christians have interpreted this verse in different ways, some believing that with enough faith, one can ask for wealth and power and receive it, while others dismiss it entirely after "trying it" and failing! Study this verse out together. What do you think God is teaching us here about asking . . . using His name in the asking . . . and that

it will bring glory to Him? (The answer probably lies somewhere in the middle of the two examples.)

6. Discuss Jesus' excitement in Chapter 14 that He is going on ahead to prepare a place for us. What do you think that means? Do you understand the disciples' confusion when He stated they ought to know where He is going and that He and the Father are one? What are your thoughts about the joy of Heaven?

7. Jesus links our love for Him with obedience in John 14:15 "'If you love me, obey my commandments.'" Why are these linked? What are some commandments that are hard for you to obey? How does loving Him help in the obedience?

8. Jesus compares us to branches attached to a grapevine in John 15. He talks about the importance of bearing fruit that lasts. He talks about how branches often need to be pruned. Share an example of a "pruning" from your life. Discuss what the fruit is that Jesus wants us to bear.

Assignment for the coming week: Read Days 36 – 40, and write out your verse and response each day. Choose one of the activities listed in the Introductory Meeting assignment for your two "days off." Come prepared to share a verse and response.

Close in prayer.

Week Eight Group Study

Open in Prayer.

1. Start by sharing with each other a favorite verse from your readings this past week. Talk about why it "mattered" to you and, if willing, share your response to the Lord about the verse.

2. Read aloud together two more accounts of Jesus right before His arrest. Matthew 26:36-56 and Luke 22:39-53. What does each account add to the story John told? Discuss how eyewitnesses all see things a bit differently. Does this hold true with the gospel accounts?

3. Review in your mind the events of that night and write a list together of every hard thing Jesus faced even before the crucifixion. Perhaps you could start with washing smelly feet! Try to find at least ten hard things. There are so, so many.

4. John spends time recounting Jesus' words about the Holy Spirit, "paraclete," the one who is called to be by our side. How does one experience this practically in daily life? Do you have an example of a time you were particularly aware of His "alongside" Presence?

5. Jesus states in John 16:33 that in this world you will have trouble. This can be hard to explain to people when they expect coming to the Lord will make life easy and comfortable. How do you live, personally, with the troubles of the world and yet the peace that comes from knowing Jesus has overcome the world?

6. What did you learn about prayer from Jesus' great prayer in John 17?

7. Have you ever been accused falsely? What is a "normal" human reaction to this? How can we learn from Jesus so that when someone accuses us unjustly, we can handle it in a godly way?

8. Jesus' conversation with Pilate is fascinating. Read Luke 23:1-24 to learn more of what they said together. Notice that Jesus said nothing to Herod, who also saw Jesus that night. What a night! Do you think Pilate was perhaps swayed a bit by Jesus? What are your thoughts on Sharon's hope that at some point Pilate accepted Jesus as Savior?

Assignment for the coming week: Read Days 41 – 45, and write out your verse and response each day. Choose one of the activities listed in the Introductory Meeting assignment for your two "days off." Come prepared to share a verse and response.

Next week will be the last meeting of our study. Take some time this week to reflect on what you have learned and come prepared to share at least two "take-aways" with the class—truths you particularly wish to remember.

Close in prayer.

Week Nine Group Study

Open in Prayer.

1. Start by sharing with each other a favorite verse from your readings this past week. Talk about why it "mattered" to you and, if willing, share your response to the Lord about the verse.

2. Share your "take-aways" with the class on the whole Bible study of John. What truths have you learned during this study that you particularly wish to remember?

3. Jesus made seven "I AM" statements in the Gospel of John. Take turns reading these out loud. Then, choose the one that means the most to you at this time in your life journey, and tell the group why.

   • I am the Bread of Life (John 6:35-51)

   • I am the Light of the World (John 8:12 and 9:5)

   • I am the Gate (John 10:7-9)

   • I am the Good Shepherd (John 10:11-14)

   • I am the Resurrection and the Life (John 11:25)

   • I am the Way, the Truth, and the Life (John 14:6)

   • I am the True Vine (John 15:1-5)

4. What did you learn about the "disciple Jesus loved" in this study?

5. What do you admire most about Jesus during His trial and crucifixion?

6. With which individual do you identify most closely as you read about Jesus' resurrection: Mary Magdalene? Thomas? Peter? John? Tell the group why.

7. In Chapter 21, we see that Peter was very interested in finding out what would happen to John. Why do you think Jesus refused to answer? When does it become dangerous to be curious about another's life journey instead of our own?

8. Finish this study by sharing what you intend to read tomorrow morning, as you continue to meet daily with the Lord.

Close in prayer.

Meet the Author, Sharon Gamble

Hello, Dear Reader!

I wish we could get to know each other over a cup of tea, my favorite way to "meet" someone! Since that's unlikely, here's a bit about me and who I am.

I love people and excitement and parties. Especially tea parties with a few close friends. I also love quiet and creating space to be still with God. In fact, I've grown to love that most of all.

I think nearly all of us know very well without any help how to be busy. But fitting in intentional time to meet with God? That can be tricky. Sharing with women ways to find that time, to know Him more intimately, and grow to love Him more deeply is my passion and my happiness and my sweet spot for sure.

Throughout my life journey, I've collected quotes that have touched me and found Bible verses that have sustained me. I've learned truths that have shaped me. All that God is teaching me in the everyday stories of life, I'm thrilled to pass on to you with a grateful heart.

In fact, God stirred me to form Sweet Selah Ministries that I might share through writing and speaking the insight, thoughts, and lessons He is teaching me, especially focused on helping women stay close to the Lord through daily times in His Word and prayer. He has amazed me by bringing a team of women alongside me to help in this journey. Now, we have others also adding their gifts of writing and speaking to this growing ministry.

My husband and I live in beautiful New Hampshire with our little teddy bear pup, Bella Grace. We belong to a great church and love hanging out with our home group every other Friday night.

In the summer, we can often be found bicycling. We have a ton of winding, quaint back roads around here, and our bikes know them all. In the winter, we tromp in the snow and build fires in our fireplace and sip hot chocolate.

We are parents to two wonderful daughters and their dearly-loved husbands, and we are Nina and Papa to an ever-growing bunch of the sweetest grandkids ever.

Along the way, through the ups and downs have come life lessons:

> I've failed and learned that failure isn't fatal.
> I've overachieved myself into basket-case status.
> I've stumbled to God in a mess and felt His arms hold me close.
> I've seen the hand of God move in miraculous ways, over and over again.

I'm still on the journey of knowing Him better and loving Him more.

I'd love to stay connected with you. Write me anytime at sharon@sweetselah.org and sign up for our weekly email that will link you to our blog, "Monday Musings," our weekly "Tuesday Talks" on YouTube, our "Sweet Selah Moments Podcast," and so much more. You can also check it all out at our website, sweetselah.org, or join in on our app, sweetselahapp.org.

You are loved,
Sharon

Made in United States
North Haven, CT
19 November 2022